**W9-BIP-581**

WITHDRAWN

Donated to
SAINT PAUL PUBLIC LIBRARY

HORIZONTAL WOMAN

Books by
Suzanne E. Berger

These Rooms *(Penmaen Press)*

Legacies *(Alice James Books)*

Horizontal Woman

S U Z A N N E   E.   B E R G E R

H O R I Z O N T A L W O M A N

The story of a body in exile

HOUGHTON MIFFLIN COMPANY

Boston   New York   1996

Copyright © 1996 by Suzanne E. Berger
All rights reserved

For information about permission to reproduce selections from
this book, write to permissions, Houghton Mifflin Company,
215 Park Avenue South, New York, New York 10003.

For information about this and other Houghton Mifflin trade
and reference books and multimedia products, visit The Bookstore at
Houghton Mifflin on the World Wide Web at http://www.hmco/trade/.

Library of Congress Cataloging-in-Publication Data
Berger, Suzanne E., date.
    Horizontal woman : the story of a body in exile / Suzanne E. Berger.
    p.   cm.
    ISBN 0-395-72668-9
1. Berger, Suzanne E., 1944–   — Health.   2. Women poets, American —
20th century — Biography.   3. Backache — Patients — Rehabilitation —
Biography.   4. Back — Wounds and injuries.   I. Title.
PS3552.E7189Z468   1996
811'54 — dc20   96-14213
                                                                        CIP

[B]

Printed in the United States of America

QUM   10   9   8   7   6   5   4   3   2   1

Book design by Melodie Wertelet

Three stanzas from "Question" by May Swenson. Reprinted with the permission of
Simon & Schuster Books for Young Readers from *The Complete Poems to Solve* by May
Swenson. Copyright 1954 May Swenson; copyright renewed © 1982 May Swenson.
"Angels of Attempted Repair" was first published as "Waterborne" in "Hers," *New York
Times Magazine*, 1994. "House of the Body" by Suzanne E. Berger, first published in
Harvard Review, Fall 1993. "Gratitude" from *The House on Marshland* by Louise Glück.
Copyright © 1971, 1972, 1973, 1974, 1975 by Louise Glück. First published by the Ecco
Press in 1975. Reprinted by permission. "The Act" by William Carlos Williams, from
Collected Poems 1939–1962, Volume II. Copyright © 1948 by William Carlos Williams.
Reprinted by permission of New Directions Publishing Corp. "Mistakes" by Susannah
Sheffer, first published in *Poet Lore*, fall 1994.

Body my house
my horse my hound
what will I do
when you are fallen

Where will I sleep
How will I ride
What will I hunt

Where can I go
without my mount
all eager and quick . . .

      — from "Question," May Swenson

Night and not night. I wake breathless
in the middle of my life . . .

      — from "The End of Mercy,"
      Dennis Hinrichsen

Contents

Acknowledgments

Special thanks from our family to my mother for her frequent visits, which relieved our confinement. And thanks to my father for his generous support. Thanks to Gail Winston, who found this book and solicited it, believed in me, gave me her editorial expertise and encouragement. Thanks to Emilie Buck Turano, who drove and drove and drove to the rehabilitation hospital.

For bringing this book to the final shore, I thank especially my friend Naomi Mittell, who was willing to help and listen in all ways; Ann Blood, for expert long-distance manuscript preparation; and Jeri Beyer, an imaginative research assistant.

I want to thank friends for striking acts of kindness, which enabled me to participate more fully in my life: Polly Bennell, for injecting joy and hope and birthday parties; Wendy Drexler, fond listener and helper; Luci Huhn, stranger when she began to help, close friend now; Debi Milligan, for so many generosities, but especially the Children's Hospital adventure; Nicki

Weiss, for gifts of laughter and camaraderie. Francy Andrews, William Daniel, JoAnne Chittick, Polly Harold, Donna Scripture, Hope Tompkins, Joe Hacker, Michelle and David Stein, stood and cheered the upward passage. Tom Villano, old friend, gave me the most important pep talk of my life. To George Cristin, thank you for wishing the manuscript on its way.

To my neighbor Mr. Spofford Crawford, I am grateful for driving; to the late Clare Ripple, for two warming helpful weeks — to these two older helpers, I offer thanks and remembrance.

For bringing me to the point where I could physically attempt to write this book, I thank all the "angels of attempted repair": Sandy Bok, Lynn Troy, Cathy Walls, Cheryl Ehrenkranz, patient healers; and later Lisa Giallonardo, who found me Paul McAndrew and Margaret Johnson, also practitioners par excellence, and Mary McCabe.

Thanks to Sally Mack and Marjorie Rekant.

For support and critical expertise, I thank my writing group, who, for fifteen years, in the words of member Miriam Goodman, have been "using the text for fellowship/studying, studying as the darkness fell": Celia Gilbert, Helena Minton, Kinereth Gensler, Connie Veenendaal, Erica Funkhouser, Kathleen Aguero, poets and wonders all.

For enriching my own work, I thank Elaine Scarry for her excellent book *Body in Pain*, from which I borrow the phrase "invisible geography" for the title for the first section of *Horizontal Woman*. I thank Eva Hoffman, whose story of immigration, *Lost in Translation*, gave me ideas for my own story of exile.

To Nora Kerr at the "Hers" column at the *New York Times*, I offer hearty thanks for bringing the first piece of this collection to light; to Kris Dahl, my agent, so much gratitude for helping me along; to Jayne Yaffe, for wonderful, precise manuscript polishing; to my editor, Janet Silver, praise and thanks for wisdom in working with words.

The MacDowell Colony, where some of this was written, served as a sanctuary.

For those I met at the rehabilitation hospital, I continue to wish you recovery. To my good friend from the rehabilitation hospital, Sylvia Willson, I dedicate "Phantom of Compassion."

Thank you, Dennis Hinrichsen, for letting me use the line from *The Rain That Falls This Far* (Galileo Press) as an epigraph.

— Suzanne E. Berger
March 1996

Prologue

Something happens, and then the world spins on a new axis.

I am standing outside a shopping mall on a shimmering fall day in Chagrin Falls, Ohio, the name of the town portentous. I bend down to pick up my child, but the bending never finishes, breaks instead into spitting lights of pain that spread over a pool of half-consciousness. A tearing is felt — heard almost — within the thickness of flesh, moving in seconds across the base of the spine. The body instantly announces: This is an important event, this is an event you will never forget. I can't get up. The asphalt is icy. Somehow I am wedged into a car. The emergency room regrets not knowing what to do.

From that moment on, I can't stand up for long without help, I can't walk for more than a few feet; using a wheelchair is difficult because I can't sit up for any useful length of time. Diagnosis is elusive. Doctors grow impatient with what they cannot see, but finally trouble is partly captured with a name. Ligament injury. But what else? Even after two years, walking is very limited, and accompanied by grinding bone-on-bone pain. Then, an expert physical therapist mines the trauma of this body, working for three hours: "I can't believe you can walk at all," he says. To get there, I have traveled in the back seat of a car, briefly in a wheelchair, then on foot, hunched over like an odd piece of human alphabet. Another verdict: hypermobile sacrum, tilted up, with severe damage to connective tissue that helps it stay in place. I had heard well that day in Ohio. Things that used to hold *did* tear, and so the disconnected sensation, like a puppet unstrung, the legs feeling loose but rigidly held like wood. It was a difficult injury to heal, not operable, unusually subject to frequent reinjury because the sacrum is always summoned for motion.

There are years of physical therapy, examinations, outpatient treatment in a rehabilitation hospital. Gradually, injury became disability, partly defined as major loss of function: walking, driving, sitting, working, not to speak of *joie de vivre* and a fixed place in the world, of certainty and known patterns of intimacy. Six years pass. The falls lost their shimmer, one by one. Finally, I could walk around a small block, I could sit for an hour.

Horizontal Woman is about life lived lying down, a kind of exile. It is about medical crises, depression from confinement that accompanies new disability like a brushfire, and about drastic upheaval in all relationships — experiences common to people faced with abrupt diminishment in health or ability. So it happens that the unexpected — an accident, the unruly cell — can change both the known exterior life and all the colors of the interior world. What does walking become, when you can't travel over the beautiful, troubling earth? A freedom taken for granted as a civil right — mobility itself — was gone, and the result was isolation and a subtle abandonment by the world of the able, the healthy, the mobile.

True, luck had left me with an injury that did not guarantee permanent disability. But the sufferer's suffering is the smallest room, and there the sufferer lives. Forced there, familiar assumptions about self and fast-moving society disappear. Accessibility is only one issue, barriers to pleasure and usefulness another. There were other questions: Who was I to myself now, without my usual capabilities, my usual physical being? How could the demanding old self, with its responsibilities and sensual preoccupations, coexist with a body that refused command? The disempowered body experiences a terrible hungry vitality, a paradox shared by many elderly and others whose bodies have betrayed them.

Differently placed on the floor, on the couch, on the ground, I appeared fallen, an outsider to be stared at. Strangely disabled, not suffering from visible damage, I did not fit in any category of illness, or "handicap," and so I was Other. Becoming Other, I could partly experience the reverberations of physical, emotional, and ethnic difference perceived as oddness in our culture, which favors the usual and the robust.

In this frightening new position, mine had to be a greatly modified parenthood, but parenthood compromised is still impassioned. I had to reshape duties, even affection, according to physical limitations, just as others must reshape behavior to fit demands of custody, or financial exigencies, or complex emotional barriers. And the vicissitudes of living with chronic pain, with daily eruptions in domestic life, added aftershock to the first shock of lost physical power.

In the way of a dark fairy tale, I was completely transformed, we were transformed. This book describes the cartography of that change, and of the many miles logged lying down during my years as the horizontal woman.

PART ONE

*INVISIBLE
GEOGRAPHY*

Running

We are branded by the images of people running through history, from bomb bursts, from pewter-colored fallout. Vietnamese children, sometimes on fire and trying to run from what is consuming them, people running in Berlin and Baghdad and Hebron, whole populations running down the long unnamed broken streets, running from mosques, from the vortices of tornadoes, from seething dogs, from the mad bull in the field. Even as they run, they seem to be in slow motion, slowly entering our interior geography. We want to turn away, we have to; but all of Hiroshima, blistered and mute, has run the miles straight into our blood, where it is packed in like the platelets we call our own.

In all these images, where are the people who cannot run? Occasionally, you see an elder being carried, but not often. What has been done with those who are not mobile? In fact, how do those who can't run escape from house fires, from floods, how do they get from the beach to their child far out there in the water?

If it came to catastrophe, man-made or natural, and we all had to flee, there'd be no time for wheelchairs, for the halt and lame, not enough strong arms to carry the crippled. And even if a few could be managed, which few?

Are those who can't run simply left, frozen or molten in their fear? I have hardly ever seen a photograph, a painting, a movie or video clip in which those unable to move on their own were present in the huge agitated exodus of streaming people. Where are they? Where would I be?

I imagine myself and others would be left behind, in the glowing streets or the greasy atomic rain. Sometimes I visit this thought on myself: it's strange to think of oneself as a Left Behind, a throwaway *by necessity* — not by cruelty or indifference — so that someone else can go about the business of surviving, or being saved.

But worse, who would run with my daughter, who would help *her* escape if my husband were not with us? If a stranger carried her to safety, to the next town, or the next country, what would happen to her watching me at the ineffable moment of my being left behind, to all the parents in the world who can't run with their babies or young children down the burning streets? What if *she,* my daughter, were left behind? This question follows me to where the soul lives, and crowds it out. There would be no soul left. Unending absence would fill the emptiness.

There's a long beach I see — or is it a road with all the trees burned off, and the houses razored away by war or hurricane or flood? Everyone is running, even though there is truly no safe place, no destination that will help anyone. Way over in the background, huddled in a clump the way the homeless gather around a steel drum for warmth, are those who must stay, the ones who cannot save themselves or others. The movie of the dream ends quietly then, the silence of true apocalypse.

In another dream, I run so gracefully I am as smooth as electricity through wires. *I sing the body electric.* People always in wheelchairs tell me they dream the same thing over and over. They are running and running when suddenly, with shock, they look down at the encumbering chairs as though, yes, surely those must belong to someone else.

But the dream of apocalypse is dreamed wide awake.

At Home

I came to see the damage that was done,
and the treasure that prevails . . .

— *from "Diving into the Wreck," Adrienne Rich*

The morning they left without me was full of hesitant snow that broke and melted instantly on the surface of my daughter's cheek. Over the phone, the metallic voices of the airline people told me the flight was about to take off, was taking off, had taken off. Since I was assuming catastrophe, I had memorized gestures, the exact color of my daughter's eyes, my husband's alert posture. A little later, when black winter light was easing into real morning, I called every five minutes to see if their plane had landed.

Since this would be the first of many trips without me — this I knew in my chilled state, with my heart iced over like a pond — for days I had prepared for it, soothed by the details of travel. I matched outfits, I counted underwear, I fussed over a treat bag for the flight, where I placed fruit dinosaurs and cheese crackers with such care that they became totemic, each piece signifying good luck, good flight. However, these were not the activities of a Good Child Keeper, Good Housekeeper, but of a woman desperate to make an impression on her child's life, to assert presence by food and by objects. Anything in my peculiar motherhood to say, See, I still do things for you, even though I can't go with you, even though I can't sit up or walk around very much. Or take you to the movies, or sometimes do anything. But I do put chocolate and notes that say "I love you" in your lunch box. I will be engraved on your childhood.

*

Let me tell you the story, child. You were the monkey torn from the hip. Suddenly, I would not pick you up, and would never again do it! When other children were being carried, warm skin to mother-skin, you'd have to walk over to me for comfort, walk to where I was lying down, and then I could hug you — you crouching, me horizontal. We stayed on the second floor whole afternoons because the stairs were impossible. Because I could do little, insignificant pleasures would be weirdly magnified so that I could be an agent for your joy. If someone brought ice cream to us, I would build it up, make a party, shout like a master of ceremonies; *Guess what we're doing today! You'd never believe ice cream!* And do you remember our so-called garden, four barrels planted with herbs, sturdy marigolds and cherry tomatoes? No grass, only asphalt, yet when it was shiny after rain the contrast between the gray and the raucous flowers was very beautiful. We'd go outside that second summer of my relapse and sample the bitter tomatoes until I had to lie down again. If I could, I'd persuade you to ride your tricycle, wade in the baby pool, or bring me presents as I lay down: everything a simulation of the real fun of playing together, of physicality. For I lay still, a stasis in your life, while you were all dynamic energy and kaleidoscope. You were amazing grace and light; I was a shadow lying across the pool. In the third summer (when you were five, we had lived with the injury for two and a half years), you didn't want to go to the garden, you were afraid of bees and flies. You were done with the bright blue containment of the pool and were, I suppose, looking beyond the confinement of those sweltering days in our back yard, beyond the confinement of my limited movement.

We would even cook with me lying down, you doing the footwork to the kitchen, me chopping vegetables on the floor for soup. When I got to the onions, nose almost on top of them, I'd start crying hard, and then the frustration of my horizontal life mixed in with the smell and I'd be crying doubly for everything. For you, for me, for the household that — though I tried to disguise it and paint over it — *was* abnormal, *was* imbalanced, *was* my body lying down at all points in your life. *Cut down*, I'd think. *Can't even make a soup*, I'd lament. *Disempowered* (though at the hospital I'd seen people with no power in their bodies, all ability having been leeched out). I'd go down so far that I never wanted you to know where. I tried everything to hide it, but in fact, cup by cup the well of the self was being emptied.

You'd grow impatient, then almost too tolerant of changed plans, and decisions based on my standing-up time. What was it like with your own desires sometimes tamped down, sometimes indulged? If you'd insist on going somewhere like a playground on a hill where I simply could not go, someone else would take you. If one part of a complex plan went askew, if someone did not show up to help us, I'd have to suddenly deny you something I'd promised. I'd lie to you, telling your disappointed upturned face, *How about that? I can't find my wallet, we'll have to get the skates next week.* I'd say, *The shoe store is closed,* when I really couldn't walk the aisles. Before you started reading, I could tell you the Cinderella movie hadn't come to town yet, that the *Nutcracker* wasn't here this year (because I could not possibly go). Where I couldn't recline, we couldn't be. Then I stopped the lies and became the mother that couldn't. You knew, and stopped asking to do things that other children did with their parents.

"If your back were better you could swim faster," you said one June day. And then I started to wait for your embarrassment about me, about my cane, my hunched-over-ness, about my lying down. I waited for shame to pass to you like a contagion. Later I dropped your papers, a stick sculpture, and your shoes all over the playground in an impossible effort to balance pain, myself, and a short abortive journey from school to car, having been driven there by a friend. As everything flew everywhere at once, you were furious, and I waited for the inevitable "you can't walk right" to drop like the heaviest stone in the well. But you finished with only an angry "you drop things all the time," and our world grew smooth to me again. You hadn't said the worst. We went to buy flowers and bread, we were happy again. *I'm just as good as any mother and don't you forget it,* I felt like saying.

*

Now they have landed in Florida. Here it's early morning still, a storm is coming and the neighbors are starting their cars for work. I'm sinking into frigid melodrama, imagining the day alone while they are hearing the palmettos clack against the warm screens of the wide-open windows. I will have a heart attack alone in this house, I will drink myself into a dangerous swerving mobility, or lie down in the snow — or was it *run* through the snow naked? — like a Sherwood Anderson character. Without the bustling, prickly needs of my daughter and her moods, my horizontalism is too clear, forced into more prominence. Without her, I am disabled; with her, a disabled mother being beautifully demanded upon. But love stretches to Florida, love's a hook that drags me up from self-destructiveness, from wanting to go down in self-pity and sorrow. It pulls me back and I settle. I start to plan the day with unwilling muscles, but the lit soul-energy of a standing-on-her-own-two-feet woman.

By now she's wanting noodles for breakfast, and the sun is a poultice for winter hurts and vulnerabilities. (In fact there's almost a northeaster there now, and she and my husband are cold and disappointed.) I'm looking to the future now through the window in the kitchen, where the snow has stopped blowing and the sun looks gray, where ice is making an exoskeleton of everything. In that future I see myself in a college admissions waiting room, lying down to accompany my daughter, who has been impressive in her interview, of course. Or I can hear her saying, *It would be better, Mother, if you didn't come with me* . . . I see her rent a fourth-floor walk-up apartment so that her independence is guaranteed by my inability to do stairs. And will I be the only horizontal mother of the bride? Will her friends soon start to ask why? Why can't your mother sit up? Why does your mother always have to lie down? Then I imagine years of companionability lopped off: the going to movies, museums, shopping, frequently the only time mothers have with teenage girls. So I just stare at the black glass, where I see a haggard shape with coffee and cigarettes too early in the morning . . .

They are far away and together: I am an oddity, now barely ever a part of going places. The child who entered this world so ungently is by now sliding on fallen hibiscus flowers, collecting old shells, demanding to run. I remember she has said things like, "When you're better, Ma, we'll go to the zoo." Once, with her face a promise she could not keep, she said, "When the circus comes again, we'll go." And I wonder if she will write stories that begin, *Once I had a mother who lay around in an old bathrobe, and said to me always, Will you please go upstairs for me? I can't, I can't.* Or stories that begin, *I don't know why my mother always made it sound like ice cream was as exciting as going to Paris or Rome.*

Snack Bar

I am the amazing living snack bar.

How did this occur, for a human woman to turn into a display of red wine, potato chips, and Knorr spinach dip in a rye bread bowl? I need a Charlie Chaplin now: would this be a place for him to enter right, his huge trousers trailing in the sour cream?

I am at a party, at my house, on the floor too near a harvest table with drop leafs braced up to hold the cornucopia of cocktail stuff and booze. So when one leaf lets go — like an arm falling in fatigue — for reasons unknown, I, being a few inches away from it but *rather under it,* as the Brits would say, I find raining down on me, without danger or fanfare, plastic cups of red wine, gin, white wine. A few potato chips fly like grease butterflies over, around, and onto me. Then in great dollops, spinach and sour cream arrive near my head, but not in my hair.

I'm laughing, knowing it begins in a closeted sorrow, knowing the edge of humiliation is being ridden, hoping no one will notice: *It's my party, and I'll cry if I want to.* But they do notice: So I keep on laughing, and then Charlie is in front of me — finally here — derby in hand, smiling, then dusting it all off me like lint, his doe-brown eyes tearing with the buried humor of it, warming me and all the world in trouble. He drinks from the cups strewn around, in a burlesque of a thirsty desert traveler, while the player piano swings a little perky tune from *Modern Times*.

And I get up, in magical transformation, with neither bruise nor stain.

New Year's Eve

"Pity. We were a good and loving invention . . ."

— *Yehuda Amichai*

I have been in the house for three weeks straight because of reinjury.

But it is New Year's, and we hope for a more upright mobile year, a new year for our changed jittery lives. You are out getting lobsters, up in Arlington; she and I are here cutting these orange papers into hearts and diamonds and dinosaurs while you're gone. I am on the floor with our daughter, in a core of domestic warmth, a small safety from the perilous outside.

While it snows and everything is softened, I'm all right; it's the sunny, overbright days I hate, days where I can see everything too clearly. Tonight is New Year's, after all, so I'll try not to be terrified about the possibility of more confinement for another year. Even the neutral word, *walking,* makes me feel an undertow, a kind of drowning. But these orange shapes, even in their silliness and frailty, beat away the gray, and for a moment I am hopeful.

She says, "I want a lobster, do a lobster," so I try to cut one out of the soft, yielding construction paper. It's difficult cutting out a lobster while lying down on your stomach, especially shaping the antennae.

Do you remember that time, in northern Maine near Moosehead Lake, when we walked into a dusty diner full of hunters? Inside there was a tank packed too tightly with lobsters, so frantic they clawed at each other. What a good and loving time for us, those years ago. There was a lambent freedom between us, as clear as that lake, an empathy of humor and purpose. Our world's too small now, with sharp angry edges, like a box with barbed wire around it. I know what you'll say: I shouldn't start remembering. We were a good invention once. I know that *was* true of us.

"But we could go canoeing then, we could do things together," I say to you all the time. "We had the outdoors. You taught me about nature." When you get back from Arlington, you set the table, cook, and serve. I drink crisp champagne and watch our daughter consider the oddness of lobster, its unpredictable spikiness, its carapace like some amazing tunnel of orange. How can something be so savage-looking and vulnerable at the same time?

Do you remember how we went canoeing in the cold at least two times a day on that vacation? It was October, and the paddles cut through the thin layer of ice, quietly cracking it. On the shore, there were red berries just laced with ice, and the mountain we could so clearly see was like a definition of *purple majesty,* O beautiful.

"We'll canoe again. Maybe not this year," you say. *Never*, I think: how would I get into a canoe, and once in it, how would I sit up? *That* beauty is over; what is to replace it?

"How about skating? Let's go to Mystic Lake tomorrow, do you want to?" I ask them. It's wonderful how I can always say, "*We* will go skating," and no one corrects me. Here's how it works, for the uninitiated, for those who haven't seen the quiet, somewhat odd, sweet spectacle. I lie on the bed made out of a thin mattress, in the back of the station wagon with the trunk open, so I can see my husband and daughter skate, even though I am freezing there. I will watch how she concentrates on her task, like a hunter with prey, trying to conquer it, determined not to fall, glancing to be sure I am watching. I'll make cocoa and sandwiches before we go; that's my contribution. We will be festive; we *will*. (But sometimes when I watch you leave with her, off to a movie or sledding or shopping, I imagine the whole bright scene without me, a moving still life, imagine you going on as usual, purposeful, self-contained, happy, a smoother voyage without my encumbering, disobedient body.)

You clear the dishes. You are so solitary in your chores. You are more solitary than you have ever been.

I put her to bed, lying down beside her for her story. This is the only way I can do it with ease, lying down, because sitting up is too painful.

She holds the raggedy paper lobster I have made her. *How about the story of our lives so far, the first part with the mother who picks the child up all the time, and the second where she can't anymore, and the child cries and sits across the room and won't kiss the mother?* Instead, I read *Cinderella*, with the glass slipper so unshatterable it always amazes me, with all the pulling and bickering over it, and the stepsisters so relentless in their cruelty that I soften the telling.

What about the first week of the New Year? I wonder. What will it bode? Who can I ask for favors this year, and who shall I pay for taking me to the rehab hospital? Can I handle a writing workshop at my house, and physical therapy on the same day? Will pain push me until I start yelling at nothing, irritated by the rasp of pain? How soon will this child feel embarrassed by me? But then I pull the blanket up to her chin, thinking, *Miraculous,* hug her, wonder whether she can feel the desperation of the hug in her sleep. *Happy New Year.* Will she be in a psychiatrist's office some day, and say, "Well, sometimes it did seem like my mother was hanging on to me for dear life." True enough, I say to the menagerie of animals in the room; they seem to multiply in the night, dolphins and gorillas and rabbits and tigers and Ernie and Bert. Do they mean too much? Their steady eyes and plush bodies hold an always predictable comfort, unaffected by mood. They are always in equipoise, amiable and soft-voiced. They are always quiet.

So, what shall it be this New Year's, a movie on the VCR, or a movie on the VCR? Shall we try to force frivolity out of its hiding place, or let it be, let it keep slumbering here? Shall we ask a whole party over here to watch me lie down, and watch as you feel more put-upon and resentful every day?

Sometimes I'm not in the real house at all. I'm on the beach, and the churning gray tide comes in, fast, and I can't walk quickly enough to get away from it. The undertow takes me out to sea. That's it: end of the story. The gulls keep on with their chattering. The sky turns black, then yellow, then blue.

"You could marry someone else, you know." I do mean it.

"Try to be more optimistic," you say, but you turn away as you say it, looking out at the confetti shower of snow.

But I will never be the person I was, the woman who canoed, the traveler, the lake rider, the sexual acrobat. I will never be at ease in this body, never believe that it's a good and useful thing, an instrument of pleasure and speed. I am not the woman you married. I am the Other, the one you wheel everywhere. The one whose shoes you tie, the one you will soon watch ascend to the second story of our house, accompanied by the extraterrestrial sounds of the new Chair-O-Later.

The undertow is with us in the room, though breathlessly I am trying to escape it, this drowning sense of sorrow and stupid self-pity. "What are we going to do?" I ask. "How can I go on like this?" I know the answer: the same way I've been doing it.

Across the room, you sit, you have heard this so many times; it's a litany you hate, purposeless, crescendoing, and always the same as before. You're wooden and remote, and I wish I could be wooden too, and want these redundant tears over quickly, so I can rise above the sodden weight of them and fly into the New Year.

We're like the lobsters in the tank, and we want to be the canoeists on the wide lake of the world, exploring. I feel like another pent-up creature in water too, a person in a Roethke poem, "stunned in the tub / with the water rising." And you're the one who loves walking, hiking. The free one, the mobile one. The water rises around me.

But we will fall asleep before the sparkling ball of the world floats into the pitch-black air and the hour of the new year begins. In New York, the new immigrants will push the trash away, paper hats will be ground into the asphalt, even used streamers will look beautiful in the new wet dark. The tourists will go home; the undertow will recede for a while; my daughter will dream of gorillas and bears; the good light glowing off the snow outside our house will disguise the gray tangle inside, and may it be a happier new year. Skating tomorrow; tomorrow a picnic in the cold, with the noise of blades cutting across the fresh ice like strokes of a pen that begins writing, "It's a New Year . . ."

Pit Bull

Physical pain destroys . . . language, bringing about . . .
a state anterior to language.

— *Elaine Scarry*

There's a pit bull next door, and he howls like a broken-down
wolf all summer. It is ninety degrees out, he's under the unforgiving sun, with a rope tying him to his decrepit house, and he
flails at the heat, sits alone in his wretchedness and hunger. No
one knows who owns him exactly — the house is either vacant
or full of scruffy transients — but he lies on his filthy rags like
a beggar-icon of city life. Now he yelps and hiccoughs in
extreme anticipation. Is someone coming to feed him some affection or scraps? We have called the MSPCA, the Angell
Memorial Animal Hospital, the dog officer, to no avail. Techni-
cally, he's not abused, they say.

When I lie in the back yard, we are separated by only a

fence; even when I am downstairs, inside my home, I can see and hear — the sun as blind and pointless as pain, the sounds of the dog, the asphalt baking, feel dirt and leaves and old cellophane and gum I can't pick up. Inside or outside, it is the whole fabric of ugliness: neglect, abuse of animal, noise. When I hear the dog, I wonder, Where's a trace of the urban fighter in this animal? The fierceness? Is it starving?

I too feel a starving, but the starving is for my old life, old mobility, old purposefulness. And this longing brings fury to the surface, bares the teeth — the ones that are inside the mouth of the soul, which are the strong and sharpest ones. But I have a new unwanted fierceness, but here in me nevertheless. For these months, I am now brought to a state anterior to human, like the dog on the other side, a dog that usually evokes fear and the paramilitary and violence.

Can I help this dog, this pitiful specimen? I lie on this lawn chair and wonder who to call, whether to feed it over the fence, fearing reprisal from people I don't know. Can I help myself here? Why do these seem like the longest summers of my life?

I am hungry for the affection of friends who have left. *They flee from me, / that sometime did me seek.* Perhaps they are fearful that I mirror what age or illness will bring. I am hungry for their freedom to walk out the door, to sit at the table for a meal, to go to the grocery store, or buy a toy, or a book, or a lotion, or stand up in line at the bank to get money, to be a *consumer.*

At night when the dog sleeps, my anger mixes with the gruel of dissappointment, and acid fear that I will be this way forever. In the daytime, I feel purer. Like that dog, I have been overexposed, but not to weather — to new disability, ending in the upheaval of my life, making me *more* of what I have only partly been before. More uncertain of outcomes, more convinced of a patternless folly, more fiercely pessimistic — negatives that were like recessive genes before. Both of our lives, the dog's and mine, are a protest, roped by pain and the irritating heat. I wonder when the muted noise inside me may erupt into some wild external noise, if fury might erupt into some antisocial action. When will my silent barking and howling be brought to the surface of sound? *Of course it won't. I am civilized. I'll be quiet, all through these summer months, and just survive.*

But that pitiful dog is mutely certain of what breed it is, and I am not. It has no way to imagine anything else. But what breed am I, if mobility is one way of looking and being, and this shock of new inactive horizontalism is another? Who am I, if I am not at all — in form or function — what I was before? I am new to me.

Last year, we had to build a tall fence to keep him away from us. But nothing can stop the howling. Though the dog frightens all of us, the sad noise of his protest makes me want some shade for him. For me, I want tenacity and some quiet hope, like shade, which will be *my* salvation from this scald of inward scrutiny.

On the Outside, Looking In

. . . so I found
That Hunger — was a way
Of Persons outside Windows.

— *from poem 579, Emily Dickinson*

Adults are not supposed to be on the floor. Adults are supposed to sit up for important conversations, sit up, not recline in a pew at weddings. So with a desire for mobility stronger and stronger, I started to look in through the brightly lit windows of normalcy, dreaming of effortless independence, of standing on my own two feet. Though a little imagination made most situations manageable — at first camping out on the bottom floor in order to avoid the stairs, or later teaching in a reclining lawn chair — for one event I could not make an adaptation. And exile was never more complete, the hunger never sharper, than when I couldn't attend services after a death in the family.

And why couldn't you go? Most people could find a way. Like a Greek chorus, partly the conscience of the community, these disquieting questions came at me: I could not because it was *beyond my imagining* to lie down at my mother-in-law's funeral. Excluded from some important joys; now, about to be excluded from formal sorrowing. Of course there were others with deeper reasons for deeper hunger, others far more damaged, at the rehabilitation hospital. The sight of contorted bodies and mute suffering was like a splash of vinegar, sharply forcing a clear assessment of my inarguable good fortune. But the comparison to greater suffering — offered so often by friends and family — was supposed to make me grateful for *only* several years of pain. And I felt guilt enough about my own rage for not being able to stand up to wash a dish, or to hug someone, rage at not being able to walk more than fifty feet.

But I was unable to do what adults do: grieve *in person*. The unables were piling up. A role was being lost to me, and with it, an identity of myself as caretaker, participant in communal experience, helper of others in mourning. Unable to participate in soothing, tending, cooking, what role was I to take in my mother-in-law's death and funeral?

For roles are the visible, nameable shape for responsibilities managed by choice, legacy, or default. Sometimes, they define the more obvious activities of the self: worker, teacher, mother, wife, writer, cable repairer. When injury or illness forces an immense change, the assumptions about those roles are knocked over one by one, like candlepins. Even when one struggles to find viable new roles — beyond the merely adaptive or subsistent — emotions regarding place in the world remain askew. One goes from being unconsciously mapped inside one's life, to being Outside, all too conscious of placelessness. Though

I had "reshaped" the roles of provider and nurturer to fit physical limitations — the relative mobility of "she-who-goes-places-but-lies-down" — I wanted my old roles back, shapely and intact. Still an active friend, more conversationally hyperactive than before, I could no longer deliver myself in person to doorsteps in times of trouble, to accompany people to important threshold events, like births, deaths, divorce court, hospital stays. Though being chosen as a mate had been founded partly on attractive self-sufficiency, I was now dependent. As a mother, my role was compromised in terms of action, but not fierce commitment. In the role of social being, it was impossible to feel comfortable or effervescent at parties, with people looking down at me on the couch or the floor. Everything was in flux, with no definition. Yet I had managed so far. We had all managed, with overtaxing amounts of extra help. Now my husband, who'd been the most help of all, was in true need and there seemed no way for me to help him.

When my mother-in-law had first become terminally ill in Buffalo, there had been no way for me to do what was required there: to give succor in a practical sense according to ancient rules of lending a hand. Cleaning, sitting to hold suffering hands, procuring food in the way people, usually women, partake in the final helping rituals that deepen a family's emotional history and expand a person's comfort in dying. This body could not rise to the occasion. If I had been able to sit in a wheelchair, for instance, I could have done many useful things. But I could offer only long-distance emotional help, not really desired in an emotionally reserved family.

How could I go there, and be the horizontal one — next to the grievously ill horizontal one — unable to carry my own share, with people having to attend to *my* needs? The sickest elder needed help to stand; how could I assist? I could help by calling her, but she was often so weak she would simply lay the phone down on her chest, and I would listen to her breathe. I was on the outside looking in to the distant house of her illness. My lifelong description of myself had included being someone who provides help, but now all I could say was, *I am so sorry I can't be there.* I did not know how to fit my competent self, with its heightened sense of duty, into a body that could not co-operate. The lifelong description was deleted.

When the time came to pay her a final visit, a deathwatch, though we didn't name it so, we didn't think the nurses would let me use the bed beside her, and I couldn't lie on the floor of the hospital. (Chorus, should we have asked for the bed?) Nor did I want to distract anyone by my physical discomfort. I stayed home.

When my husband and daughter left at six A.M., I watched a movie, a sense of unreality drifting throughout the house, un-real as my still new self, *not* there in Room 210 of Buffalo General, where I saw my husband armed with crayons and stickers, trying to help our six-year-old daughter with a good-bye she did not know she was saying. I began to see myself in the third person: she, the person who was not there to comfort. See that person back in Boston on the outside of collective family sorrow. See that mother not there, her own child far away beside her mute grandmother's bedside. Role by role by role, a further diminishing, or so it seemed. And finally, see the mate — she who hardly considers herself one now — abandon the husband.

Three weeks later my mother-in-law died on a warm September night. We knew I wouldn't manage the service at the funeral parlor because there were no benches or pews. And for the later burial of her ashes, I couldn't imagine lying down on the ground, the pure unintentional irreverence of it. So the breaking sense of self broke again. Not being there to fulfill the shape of mourner seemed disrespectful, a failure to give witness. *Don't blame yourself*, the Chorus might soothe, but doesn't unjustified blame taste as cold and bitter as blame we *do* deserve?

My daughter didn't go: without me, who would take care of her there? At home, we investigated her grandmother's death from the child's point of view, startling but manageable. *Do they take all the blood out of the body?* On the vital inside of her questions, my motherhood and my mourning were fluid and active. I helped my child with her beginning grief, the angry adult look of consternation on her face, her sky-colored eyes occasionally growing stormy with doubt. *Do you see the dead person? How do you lie down when you die? Is the body the same size when you die?* Guiding her toward answers, I was snug in my role. But I was outside the chilled group under the crisscrossed power lines of upstate New York. Sometimes now, when I play my interior movie of those mourners together, I wonder if there should have been a woman lying on a mat in the funeral parlor, or even outside near the plain burial marker, paying tribute to a lost bond under the unforgiving gray sky.

The Chorus does not answer my wondering.

House Tour

I am this body & the weather all year round.

— *from "Wings," Philip Schultz*

You walk into the story partway through the plot. Say it is almost spring, with all the introverted windows of winter flung wide open to let in the strangely pure urban air, even with its trace elements of Monday garbage, sesame oil, ripe budding bushes, and, somewhere, cardamom and axle grease. Look over to the right, through the window that directly faces the corner of Kenmore Street and Winwood, then gauge the distance from the old wraparound farmers' porch of this house to that corner, which may soon be turned by a student; or a professor saving money by living here; or new teenage parents with carriages of babies and groceries; can-pickers who work the streets like emissaries from a haunted future, scarved in gray, darting here, digging there, for bottles and salvageables. Now imagine a winter day, a few hesitant footprints marked in the light, bare fall of snow, as the art of walking takes place just to that same corner: the bold goal, then the goal captured. But how to return? And so the defeated look back from the corner toward the house, the ambiguous sanctuary with the too familiar couches and floors inside — the house not left for weeks, for those weeks the walls the only view.

Being stuck there, out at the corner, is now a permanent part of the view in each season, belonging to the corner as the street signs do, just as a neighbor's death becomes part of the neighbor's house. As though weather and light, like a lathe, still turn the same human winter shape out every day, the struggle still continuing in a rampant spring, in the fall: *How to get back?*

And the glowing house is often silent, with little lively sound. An uneasy quiet fills the rooms most days, just as confinement seems to swell with emptiness, even though the windows allow restless eyes to escape outward. The house can seem like an aquarium with seasons inside, moving slowly through like plant filaments.

In the driveway now slick with black ice, slated over with crisp nodes of snow, white on white, there's a white station wagon parked close to the house. The car was purchased for its split back seat, so that a long single foam mattress may be laid as a bed, so that there will be breaks in the monotony, from waiting through the years for mobility, waiting through time that is slow and thickened, and contorts like silly putty — waiting that is impatient and unnatural.

Meanwhile there are some trips out in this car, some tentative meandering drives. From the house, part of the mattress may be seen, a bright tropical flower-strewn sheet flung over it, a splotch of color in the white cheek of winter. In the car, promises of adventure take flight unreasonably.

And here is the living room, the room over-lived in, which every three months or so becomes the dining room, changed for the illusion of changed venue, for calming the interior vision gone both agitated and worn from sameness; as though changing the furniture will change where pain resides, or lessen its intensity. Often, more often than in other houses, paintings are transposed, photographs switched, throws and pillows moved from here to there and back, trailing their memorized pattern behind. The colors of the walls are changed too because there are the low percussive notes of years spent mostly in these two rooms; the eyes need to escape from visual sameness, and so are deliberately rescued by yellow, or a dimensional white. And now the living room/dining room is a pink terra cotta, ersatz Italian fresco, a color warm but not fevered. Once there were many slashes of approximate color, in a delusionary attempt to find an intensity that would please unerringly through the seasons, without becoming a flat maze of self-inquisition. Why such skewed perception, bad taste in color, pretentiousness in a house in this modest neighborhood? Light makes *this* pink almost a dark Necco-wafer color at dusk but in the day suggests an exotic other landscape, where a panoramic world of change and richness occurs. Whatever the color, in whichever space named dining room, a double bed is placed close to the dining room table, a bed first used for eating, resting, playing cards lying down, for sleeping on the first floor, for the smooth music of physical therapy's score; then for reading and playing children's games, then, much later, for sleeping away from conflict and harsh mutual decisions, for brooding in summer, with the door to the small porch wide open to clarity or solution.

And all of this too difficult to explain to those who wondered, Why a bed here? Why in the dining room? Much about the house is too mysterious to explain. But in these two rooms, happiness too: birthday parties have passed, trailing their wonderful torn bright streamers and debris, emphatic footfalls of toddlers and the warming scent of friends, then trampings of the older child's independence. But also there was too much other time passed in boredom and frustration, marked by invisible fists hitting and crumbling the plaster in protest: one hit for each year horizontal, each year of immobility, each year now gone. Meanwhile, steady and needful, the old black cat of the house shadows around corners, nestles into arms to comfort and be comforted, a piece of punctuation for the long run-on sentence of many days, the cat constant and fat, lavishly folded in upon itself, soothing; love *it is* from animals, in their suspension of all judgment and in their soulful demands.

Up to the second floor, you find a staircase of unsurpassed but possibly redeemable ugliness, the wood varnished with a cheap, shiny stain called, variously, "Tobacco Spit Juice," "Baby Poop Lite," and just "ugly." There has been time only for maintenance in this house. A fifties embossed carpet spreads up the stairs like a yellow and Tang-orange stain. Then behold: waiting like a beast to be summoned to labor, the brown Naugahyde chair elevator goes up and down many times a day, and is nicknamed, sometimes fondly, sometimes bitterly, in addition to the Chair-O-Later, The Electric Chair, the Spielberg machine, and the Magical Mystery Chair. The plain given name is Chair Elevator, Whittaker Company. Indian blankets have been tossed over the top for decoration, and then cushions, (thrown off in transit), then swatches of incongruously bright fabric — nothing works, it is basically undecoratable but loyal. The machine carries up, then down, with the flick of a hand switch, with a noise like a spaceship, a noise that beguiles and thrills older children, who relish the slow rides on it, but has made smaller children scream and hide — so odd, so identifiably otherworldly, with a creaky, industrial submusic to it. This chair giveth and giveth and giveth. There were two years at least when the chair should have lived here, but hesitation and denial lived here first, kept it rented, never purchased.

The installer patiently explained that maintenance involved applications of baby powder to the thick rubbery wires that carry the chair. Baby talc? There were jokes: Do you diaper it too, rock it to sleep? There was much real laughter; laughter, an unusual spring burbling up cold and clear, but not later when almost all able-bodied adults refused to try a ride, as though fearing contamination, or bad luck for body parts. The rides were offered in the spirit of sharing the amazing grace of up-ward ascension without physical effort, the almost bodiless floating feeling, despite seeing oneself as the elderly person in the ads, going up, with the sound of flying saucers and flying witches. This mechanism of freedom and bliss mixed with the other gritty noises of the house, but it was so loud it could not be used when others slept. So it slept, too, unlikely gift, closing one half of the house down.

When it finally is gone years later, long past the time of still needing it, the orange carpet will be half clean on one side, where the long, talc-dusted wires were, very dirty on the other, from years of shoes and boots and slippers, millions of steps up and down. And the silence the chair leaves, though that silence means strength and ability, is fierce. What if it's needed and it's not there?

At the top of the stairs, you turn right into an unfinished

bathroom, where frequently there is the silvery music of a shower, possible for only a few seconds, baths abandoned entirely for six years despite their singular calming effect, their way of turning the motor of frantic thinking into a still pond. But to get into a bathtub you must rely on innate cooperation of neuron and muscle — and the everyday grace of plain coordination and self-assurance — the easy contortion of the whole body. Of course, some sort of crane could have been procured, but wasn't. In the bathroom, the window is often open to let in the spicy spring air, or winter briskness, as the seasons pass irrevocably. These years were to be gotten through: the impending hours to be endured, the child enjoyed and cared for well, everything shuttled through, the weaving and unraveling of daily life continuing on.

To the left is the child's room, with Legos all over the floor like a scattering of spores from the same strange civilization the Chair belongs to; with Barbie torsos separated from Barbie legs; the humming music of a child's concentration on a Monet water lily puzzle, pieces now scattered across the floor; heavy curtains trying to flutter in the winter sun, in the first autumn gusts, in the regular repetitions of the summer fans, in the first spring wildness. Rubber bands and hair bows are on the floor, and an opulent waste of toy parts, with the Claw in the corner, always ready for use in such matters as picking up these toys, old towels, in obsessive attempts to neaten this house. The Claw is simply a long-armed reacher with a magnet on the end so that no one has to bend, a device sold in those forlorn stores with wheelchairs and bedpans in the dusty windows (catheters, hospital beds, shower stools, enema bags, hidden inside), a store that feels like a prosthesis itself, added on, not natural. (Bless it.) One at a time, pieces of anything can be picked up with the help of the Claw — that black checker piece, this stuffed animal with velour ears — then returned to its rightful place in the corner. One thing by one, the whole populous floor is cleared, the Claw held fast in impatient hands, hands that win the Gold Medal in Assisted Picking Up. There is satisfaction, embarrassed pride, on certain days when other thinking is not possible.

Across the hall, you see into an adult room with an adult miasma of newspapers, books, pill bottles, heating pads, pencils, scarves, bright rugs, a bed flat on the floor (easier to rise from), bathrobes around, nightgowns put away, for there is never a whole day spent here in bed, or in the bedroom — deliberately, defensively. These walls are painted often too, each time a shade chosen in an effort to make the room more hopeful, less full of the resonance associated with surrender to new darkness, or with destructive habits of responding to pain. That music has drifted into the corners, joining dust motes, or into cornices above the door, so often slammed for emphasis in argument. Even the present color, butter yellow, feels shadowed, almost greenish at times, mostly at dusk, especially after doctors' appointments. In this room you can see clearly out the windows kept immaculately clean, for months are spent considering the brown leaves, the ice kimonos on the arms of the trees, the crows: the reputed "solace" of nature as a last resort for the confined eye and the damaged sense of self.

If you look up, you can see of the plaster ceilings, starred with random flecks of gold metal that fall sometimes, ceilings to contend with, viewed constantly. The visual staccato of this gold means the eyes can never rest; there is no constellation or pattern to follow. Full of good workmanship and aesthetic principle at the time, the house was renovated in the sixties; these ceilings now should be plastered over. And *if* there is a music for the whole ceiling-skin of the house, it is Philip Glass, further flattened, the same note played over and over.

Up in the attic, up a stairway even still too steep to climb, is an assortment of hard foam shapes, pillows for knees and legs and back, enough shapes to make a Stonehenge there, with the old useless orthopedic shoes waiting for a new owner, borrowed crutches, brace-belts, and on top of an old trunk, some letters never sent. If you opened one fat envelope — one of many addressed to the same place — you could read "That I begged you to come see me and you *wouldn't,* even though you were in New York, so close to Boston, that was the last straw. Somehow I didn't think that winter I'd make it. Couldn't you have helped a little?" and beside these piles of letters, old metal fans — tall ones on pedestals, short chubby ones for tops of tables. And imagine all of their dusty faces whirling like tin sunflowers, trying to push the melancholy air out, so that the house could breathe, so that the owners could breathe again clearly too, and go on doing what they had to do, after the middle of the story.

Perspectives

From this angle on the floor, I look upward to people looking down on me, see the crescents of fat under chins, observe the vulnerable place where socks do not quite meet pant cuffs. Strangers try not to stare, to hold at bay their animal instinct to flee the weak or the injured. At airports or train stations people have thought I was derelict or crazy or maybe homeless; only the dispossessed lie on floors, children lie on floors, dogs lie on floors, tiles lie on floors, but adults? *What's that woman doing over there?* a security guard said at the airport. *Dunno, leave her alone. Must be drunk.* With friends inside my house, being down here upsets a balance of conviviality, of the *whereness* that grounds a conversation. I am always looking up, as though younger or subservient. Outside I live down with mother-dirt, grass, the asphalt of the city. Wherever I go, I lie down with my mat. *Hey, lady, what the hell you doing down there?* says a child on a city playground. *You sick? You tired?*

Rugs love me, are intimate with me. I know their relative quality, their deepest secrets, the quietness of their lint and various stains. The ones with pads underneath are the friendliest, the cushioning a balm for the spine. The dust is comforting down there on the floor, as is the discovery of old marbles, Hershey's Kisses, thumbtacks. At home, I look up at too white ceilings, at water stains that are like Rorschachs, cobwebs like soft gray jewelry for the high corners they decorate. Most of the time I am at home, I am about eight inches tall, the height of my width lying down sideways on the floor. I am a flatland, and the world is mountainous. For instance, when I rise for the occasion of kissing my child as she stands on a stool, so that I won't have to bend, it is ecstasy. The odd angle of self meets the curve of normal love: the curve of her cheek meets the angle of my unusual motherhood. I am momentarily in the land of the upright.

Traveling in the car, I am the queen of segment perception as I lie on the bed in back. I see the parts of things, the parts framed by the half of the window where I look out, and from these I extrapolate the whole. If one color of a sooty urban sunset can be seen, I can imagine the whole spectrum of odd mauves and metallic brown-grays spread out over the sky. Show me a punk's torso through the window, with black leather and studs and zippers, and I'll show you the torn pants below, the angry face above. I'm missing the way it really is, everything is broken into these pieces or planes of perception, something a painter might choose. But I don't choose it.

Lying in the back of the car, I can't lean forward to look at the faces of the people talking up in the front, so I work harder to interpret the hues and tones of voices, the various quick motions of their heads. The top of my head is at the back of the driver's neck, so there's no way for the driver to engage me either. I never have any idea of the real weather of the conversation, cloudy in one person's face, open and clement in another's. So I stare at the pocked vinyl ceiling of the car while others talk, and I imagine the subtexts occurring in front, imagine the revealing gestures. Sometimes they forget I am here, and then I am an invisible traveler.

When I have to stay at home, which is most of the time, the hunger for the whole perspective grows acute. Others, those who go places, who can see the whole world, are full of dimension and thrilling motion; I am mostly in sleep's posture, but not an invalid. So when someone goes out for a gallery opening, a concert, a new movie, I try to force them to bring everything home to me in excruciating detail. What color exactly was her dress? Was the meal vegetarian? When the event is too desirable — the aquarium, an opera, a circus — the bitterness at being left behind waxes like an unwelcome moon in our house, casting its bad light everywhere. (When they leave, I turn on the TV: self-pity is all, and I cannot eat or talk or call anyone.) There is only the imagined iridescence of costumes, the beauty of new noise not heard by me. From a distance, the world where they go seems rich with motion and bonhomie, its appeal almost erotic. So when they return, if everything is not described with passionate vigor, I go into despair for specifics. *Can't you tell me more? Can't you remember the name of that fish?* And the details demanded exhaust and anger the detailer.

Perhaps after one of these outings, after one of our scenes, I decide to take my daughter for a treat, a quarter of a block to the corner store — to apologize for being cranky about not being told enough. (Of course, once in a store, I usually grow panicked, because I still can't stand up well, and then I rush her through everything, so that what should be leisurely becomes messy with anxiety.) But we *do* go, and as we inch along, there's the imagined array of fierce dogs I can't run from, strangers who might snatch her, all fast-forwarded before my slow-motion body. When we have to cross the street, it is like crossing a firing line; I hold my cane across us like a thin, insufficient shield. The cars are bullets. We try not to get hit, but moving this slowly makes us perfect targets.

When we get back to our house, I decide I should have stayed home after all, because I have only succeeded in giving my daughter the great gift of abundant fear about the danger in everything. And omnipresent panic. And overvigilance about hazard, against which I cannot defend us. That night I will dream of being powerful, full of speed, saving her from huge cosmic danger, and then awake to the gritty daytime knowledge that I am even afraid to stay alone with her at night (I could not run downstairs if there were a fire). That night I might also dream of wearing high heels, even though I never wore them or wanted them before. In dreams I am whole and competent, I am never horizontal. I am tall: I am myself the whole perspective, and the dogs of the world cringe.

PART TWO

REHABILITATION

BLUES

House of the Body

The electricity fades in you, the shades are drawn.
Where are the windows to look through,
where are the mice of play?

There are vestiges of lost motion in you,
and filaments of desire:
the world constricts to the size of pain.
The television blinks like a flickering nerve.

Morning comes to you like an exclamation,
at the table where you eat self-pity, cold,
where you have no inner light to mix with it.

Consider love, how it has fallen on its knees
with the steep fall of the body.
Consider night, how it will soothe the ruined house

with birds, comets, all things
swift and phosphorescent,
how they extend their wings
over the stiller life of sleep.

If you live in a house of the body which has become a
house of chronic pain, you are welded and wedded to it —
all the while wanting like hell to escape. In an age overly
committed to a mind/body doctrine of consuming unity and
determinancy, pain provides a dramatic contradiction to current thinking. Like many elements at odds with each other,
the "dysunion" pain creates can last and last. Because what the
mind desires so passionately — cessation of pain, resumption
of activity — the body cannot requite. And the pure possibility of free thought, infinite thought, is set starkly against
the confinement of the body, now unreliable, now restrain-
ing the mind like a quirky harness. Estranged and burdened, the two labor to make it through the hours, traveling
inch by inch through the miles of a day. For instance, if I
try to set the mind free to drift like a kite, away from body-
matter-that-is-me, it comes back down, a barge weighted with
the scrap of the body. Though I command relaxation in the
body, as I have been ordered, for the body to be in kinship
with itself, it can't obey. Over and over there's disagreement,
rebellion, incessant claustrophobic conflict. Mind says, *I want
you to leave me alone, or go run, or get out off the couch, or . . .*
Body says, *I can't, pain won't let me. So you shut up.* Mind
cannot, so ultimately it is unfree, or free only to explore ob-
sessively the injury or trouble or illness, and the whole self
is trapped by all four paws in the woods. Not only is there

the absence of the freedom to traverse the wide world, but mental freedom is ruined too, as the mind becomes more preoccupied by the body's limitations, snagged on one simple theme, *I want, I want,* until the world, the house, is reduced to the size of pain. With always drawn shades, the house is in stasis and perseveration.

Then, of course, as is usual in perverse human nature, what's completely impossible holds out the strongest lure of escape from those small rooms. You want to do those things that are the hardest: the more treacherous and inaccessible, the more seductive. I started to tune in to exotic travelogues on TV, almost carnally craving the sight of the Himalayas in Nepal, feeling myself riding a donkey with a Sherpa beside me. Ready to book a flight to Africa for one of those genteel safaris, I'd remember that someone lying down could not possibly survive those wild jeep trips over the veld to see the rampaging lions. Even a look at a white Italian hill town, with tourists managing the cobblestones (to me as graceful as Nureyev), could make me weep, for I correctly knew the freedom to walk like that would not be mine for years, maybe ever. Polaroid ads of people, lithe and mobile American families, picnicking by a stream in the Rocky Mountains, could almost weaken with envy, make me dive into melancholy, for how would anyone without maximum agility ever get *there?* And running ads, ads for Reeboks, for health consciousness, even for the cutesy little shavers for the legs that run, all of those were the worst, as I would watch them on purpose and greedily, in spite of what happened when I did. For I had started to dream of running through fields, running through foreign cities, precisely I think because I would never run again — not *from* danger, not *to* joy or safety. In my dreams I would even race and leap. In the dream life, a healthy middle-aged woman is always running, though not very swiftly, with her young daughter through the pages of their history, through a volleyball court, through a castle. But she does run, in that place where the body has not yet taken its steep fall to disability.

The grace of acrobatics, birds swooping onto telephone wires, curves of geometry, lithe skaters: all became magnets for laserlike energy, as I watched them on TV, sighted birds outside (though I had never been in the least interested in bird-watching), stared at the twistings and archings of gymnastics, as though I were seeing for the first time the far mutational possibilities of the clever body. *Amazing grace* did not begin to describe the wonder of the radiant "obeyments" of the body to the mind's beckoning which I saw on the mats. *Miracles.* In ballet, all flexion, pirouette, and leap were gathered into something not really built of muscle, tendon, practice: it was something angelic, or in the realm of physical theology. It seemed like a holy condensation of intent, and the body's recitation of the wonders on the earth. *Miracles.* Even a comet would curve like my spine could not; even the effortlessness of mosquitoes landing on flesh was noted, inspired envy.

Because with disability or injury — anything that destroys body-ease — much fades in you, while all motion, refined and mundane, achieves an electric phosphorescence that stretches over all other people's travels in the world. There's even a glow to the imagined freedom others have with their bodies in sex.

You're like a voyeur, but you can't picture the freedom *for your-self*, in your own body, because you will always fear pain with any abrupt new movement.

Confidence fades and pain bleaches the color of your self, even making the real skin ashen. At the rehab hospital, many people have a pale, waxy mask of pain on their faces, expressionless, with overly animated eyes shining out. When I look in the mirror on bad days, my skin is the color of pared potatoes. And my body now has a previous self; pain has aged me more dramatically than chronology could have done, and I am weary of carrying around a previously hearty self. Sometimes the electricity in me has felt gone completely, parched and faded a continual way of life. But now there are stretches of Technicolor.

*

Is there nothing optimistic to say? No benefits to the solitude or confinement? Nothing good that was harvested?

Try, as they say in cheerful pamphlets, to make pain your companion. But pain gives almost nothing back, gives only endless time. Its only gift is cessation; it is encoded only with potential relief from itself. It is always the large, overpainted foreground, with tiny people receding back into it, people who often prefer pain drugs (called killers with good reason) or the still life of sleep, or booze; or acquire messianically charged visions of overcoming pain. But we can always rise up with energy and evangelical fervor to recite in a litany all that pain can take away. In this commitment to shouting out the losses, people will often find their way through it, using that same dark simmer of energy for their lament. Our collective dark

ode to pain might begin: O taker of transportation and liveli-
hood, taker of ease and of full parenthood, taker of inner and
outer space and the freedom to explore it, taker of known maps
for the psyche, taker of humor that begets friendship, taker of
friendship that begets warmth, taker of sex and the hopeful
light at the hopeful window, taker of delight in the walking
rituals of the seasons, taker of smooth self-fulfillment, taker
of travel and geographical discovery, taker of appetite, taker
of interior color and vibrancy, taker of laughter. Maker of
cynicism and the bitter word, the turning away of others,
creator of strangers called *self-hate* and *give up*, who move
in the house of the body, maker of self-pity that begets the
soul of depression, that begets smaller and smaller rooms of
exile . . .

*

*What about the soul? If the body is the temple in ruins, in con-
finement?*

What about the soul? Not Emerson's Over-Soul, not the
soul as irradiated by St. Theresa's ecstasy, but more like Spin-
oza's persistence of essence, like a transparent heart always
beating *inside* the personality. Chronic pain seems to starve the
fleshy part of your soul, and its generous perceptions, while
self-pity persists in feeding it the wrong stuff. You can just sit
there eating it, of course, but the room grows darker and lone-
lier around you with each meal, each season passing *outside*
your life with banners, bells, and whistles. Because the prepon-
derance of dark self-regard pushes others away, and makes a
boring diet. Also a relentless dominatrix, pain makes you cringe
from the constant self-referring. But because you do feel *ruined*,
especially at first, it's almost impossible to do otherwise, though

you promise yourself not to complain in front of others. However, the incessant effort not to bemoan fate, not to be openly anguished, makes for a drastic inhibition of the self, so that the voice attempting to be cheerful will come out sounding tinny, with a kind of empty brightness, like rhinestones. An effort that, I believe, pushes confined people back into themselves, alone at the table, the inner light and energy having been spent on the work of not appearing depressed, not letting self-pity show. Self-referring then is traded for self-effacement, not a fair transaction at all.

*

"The merest schoolgirl when she falls in love has Shakespeare or Keats to speak her mind for her, but let a sufferer try to describe a pain in his head . . . and language runs dry."

— *Virginia Woolf*

The house of the body in pain is furnished with inexact metaphors that resist tidy medical labeling, and with approximate descriptions of extreme states. You find yourself at a loss, with language running dry just when needed most — that is, when explaining an internal teeming microcosm to the medical world, the physical therapy world, *and* to the macrocosmic world of relationship to others in general. Since pain can neither be verified nor denied in many cases, the person in pain is doubted — are you malingering or overdramatizing? — which only then amplifies the pain. With only vivid, but subjective comparisons to "defend" ourselves with, we can hardly communicate at all. I remember saying, "It feels like my back is a radio someone took apart and put back the wrong way," to the wondering disbelief of the doctor attending to me. I wasn't being clever or imaginative. It *was* to me like a broken radio with the wires randomly tossed back into the case. Of course, no one could understand such poetics, but there was no other way to speak. Slowly there is a temptation to shut up entirely. Often, I compared my spine to a steel cable, but one that couldn't bend. Intimately part of me, yet divorced from me — *it* hurts, not *I* hurt — the lower spine became an entity punished by harmful instruments; a steel cable being hammered on, or pinched, or hit with a rock, all animated comparisons. But these were comparisons that set me apart, did not conjoin me to the world of healing, where precisely described medical statements, like verbal X-rays or CT scans, would have enlisted help more efficiently. "I feel like my legs are about to faint," I said for years. Who among us, even in the Club of Pain, could understand that? The privacy of pain finally encloses the person like a deep moat.

And the psychological states of the isolated person, the person who is doubted and can speak only in these strange tongues, are often expressible only by comparison. With any kind of depression, people commonly speak of being in a fog, or underwater, or surrounded by darkness; they will not simply list the eight signs of Big Trouble, sleeplessness, loss of appetite, et cetera. And so, I began to associate moods with lower forms of life, with amoebas, slugs, not because I hated myself, but rather because their attributes — like aimless movement, quiet protoplasmic struggle, a kind of body blindness — resembled what I was feeling, not despicable, just mute and dark. "How can you say you feel like a slug?" people would ask. I could never explain that it wasn't a cruel or belabored comparison, just the truth: another illustration of the failure to communicate in an acceptable comradely way. It wasn't ugly; it just was. In me the shades were simply drawn against conventional descriptions of my body. Is it so for others, too?

*

> "When one hears about another person's physical pain, the events happening within the interior of that person's body may seem to have a remote character of some deep subterranean fact, belonging to an invisible geography that, however portentous, has no reality because it has not yet manifested itself on the visible surface of the earth."
>
> — *Elaine Scarry*

Without a common language for sharing the deepest experiences of the self, isolated with a "subterranean fact," the person in chronic pain, or the person painfully disabled, can feel like an immigrant in a new world, on real terra infirma. Horizontal, I began to operate like a stranger in the world, uneasy, too willing to please, trying too hard to blend in, though everyone was looking down on me. We could have been two species: those who move around and those who lie down. They were the natives, I the intruder.

Just as the immigrant finds solace in immigrant enclaves, so the rehabilitation hospital was a refuge, but for many of us only a few times a week. The vast Other World, the *visible surface of the earth,* of health and mobility and camaraderie, loomed fearfully on the in-between days. This foreign land was where I and others had to live after all; it confused and angered us. So much was taken for granted there; so much was shared by the inhabitants who traveled so gracefully through it and walked as casually as they breathed. Who were we, where was *our* world?

As the essayist Eva Hoffman explains about her sense of displacement, when moving to Canada after emigrating from Kraków, the center of the world moves, as reference points "do a flickering dance." The body is a world; the reference points are motion and self-knowledge, physical habit and predictability. When those points "flicker," the owner is in existential dislocation, and as Hoffman also notes, there is "no longer a straight axis anchoring the imagination."

But where can that "immigrant" go to find surcease besides the hospital, when the inner "invisible geography" places the geography of the body in another country? To some outer reaches: in many cases, the arctic outreaches or hinterlands called Trance Hours and fantasizing about final catastrophes as an escape from pain. Trance Hours are made of prescribed drugs; whether painkillers or antidepressants or tranquilizers, their purpose is to mute psychic pain, bodily pain, anxiety — sometimes all. The drugs giveth and the drugs taketh away. They give by neutralizing hellish sensations, of whatever content. For the "flickering dance" of psychic displacement, the drugs offer an evening out; for pain, a quieting from the usual noise.

Drugs can protect from the danger of self-defeat that brews in an environment overly heated with pain. And relief from what I call the undertow, which causes a loss of balance, ending in the strong pull toward feeling drowned in pain, pulled out to sea, *finito*, barely able to surface for daylight, for food, people, responsibility. They can help you rise from that undertow to the rational surface of everyday life, even if you are a little "tranced." But drugs also can take away the sharpness of joy or healthy anticipation, when those clear emotions do surface; or the anxiety of disappointment or sorrow, which may sometimes serve as dark motivators.

Drugs muffle, drugs mute, drugs help. In a way, drugs taken for a long time in order to soothe slowly grow an eggshell around the brain . . . a fragile barrier for protection, but also a barrier against the dramatic strength of feeling in general. What lies outside the ruined house — stimulating and tempestuous or thrilling — must pass through the eggshell, and by the time it has passed, it *is* less, diluted and lighter. If an experience *out there* were to weigh ten pounds of feeling, it would be reduced to four by the time it goes through the eggshell. Sometimes the accurate experience of pain and pleasure is remembered as though occurring very long ago, and through thick gauze.

But the immigrant is forced to take any measure that creates a nest of peace as relief from the "deep subterranean fact" of new disability, or the mood that accompanies it, ambling alongside like Churchill's "black dog" of depression. Often, there is nowhere to go but inward. And if the drugs make the inward bearable, why not have them?

For some of us there's also a sense of placement and "centerment," in self-aggrandizing fantasies of oblivion.

When purposelessness and futility moved in, apparently permanently, and my mind was crowded out, I "flew" to those places, where balm and safety were offered. I never really meant to leave, but the seductive lively procession of fantasies occupied many confined "horizontal" hours. And yet my very disability, I figured out one night, would botch what I *really didn't want to do anyway*, my imaginary plan of getting myself drugged out just enough to "escape" to a psychiatric hospital, or at least aggressively gather the sympathy of everyone around me. I had thought a few times of this calculated overdosing, really underdosing in the beautiful weeds near a pond not far from the route to the hospital. But then I remembered the vagrants there, the ones who slept and ate and made the sheltered inlets their dwellings, and how, if a dangerous one found me — all dazed and out of it — he'd take my watch and money, hit me over the head, and actually kill me dead, which I had never really wanted in the first place. End of fantasy. What I really wanted people to understand was how pain had subsumed my life and the I that used to be.

But it did not feel that way, did not feel like "lesser suffering." In my body's immigrant world of lost references of motion, I still lived in disbelief that I couldn't walk more than a few hundred feet. And in wonderment, I still saw myself being pushed in a wheelchair as though from a galactic distance, in exile. There such fantasies and dread, rehearsed over and over, were like fixed axes (you can fantasize, then you can stop), certain and predictable where the body was not. But at night, the ruined house was soothed by broken sleep and sometimes drugs, but not except in poems visited by things swift and phosphorescent. Those beautiful things lived out beyond the window where I looked: birds gracefully flying, children running without effort, adults embracing while standing up on their own two feet. All this would be gazed at and longed for and loved from afar like islands of joy viewed from the shore.

Entering Paradox

Here I am on a too bright April just after my forty-third birthday, the sun overexposing all the weary gas stations, the Friendly's, the skimpy mall with only a Toys "R" Us and a boarded-up Pizza Hut, as we drive up a long, seemingly infinite driveway with bumps and potholes I can feel slamming into my spine like thunder as I lie in the car. We pull up to a place that could be a town reservoir building, a sewage plant, housing in Oklahoma for retired cowboys: an anonymous building, made of new bricks painted to look old, with nothing to demarcate the blank facade except balconies. I count them: twenty-six balconies.

At the front desk, laboriously cheerful silk flowers; there are four bouquets, some April Fool's cards, and some Marlboros. The sharp-jawed, overly tan receptionist offers a have-a-nice-day-whatever-is-killing-you smile: "Who did you have an appointment with, hon?" I hope I have an appointment with mobility, hon.

For that is why I have come to this rehabilitation hospital on a hill, this paradox with its hell of countless wheelchairs lining the halls, their obviously agitated occupants whispering and waiting, all ages and all kinds of broken and damaged. And it is the promised heaven of possibility — the end of pain, or the arduous beginning of walking, or the use of a new limb — the heaven that is this place of healing and mostly good intention. Here is one mass of suffering people, all brought together by their desire for normal life, usual movement.

The paradox is decorated in beige, and the beige directional arrows are outlined with gravy-brown: this way for Prosthetics OT, Pool, PT, Stress Clinic. My wheelchair moves slowly over a chartreuse rug flecked with a pepper of black and brown, like a tossed salad ground into the floor. In the physical therapy room, the primary colors of exercise balls wham against the monotones, punctuating everyone's routine like neon — happy colors for a change.

Give us a break, hospital decorators, for this looks like planned bleakness, bleakness with a vengeance. Did someone work hard to make the defeated environment reflect us, be the color analog for our inner selves when we finally arrive here? The older people sigh and moan. One says, Oh, Jesus, Mary, and Joseph, Mother deliver me. The young people, or relatively young, wait in disbelief and in grave hope.

Welcome to the Halt and Lame Club. You have entered the gates of heavenly promises. It is hellish here, but you have earned it. You may ask a few questions: Why are all these people in the hall, slumped over, looking abandoned? Waiting? Why is that

*young woman with blank, wandering eyes over there, in her pink
chenille bathrobe, with that young child so urgently trying to talk to
her? Why is this club exclusive? What are the dues?*

Why am I in a wheelchair, I still ask myself about this
body — so like me and not me — this body that feels like an
actual material burden: a sack of flour, a load of laundry. Why
have I taken this long netless fall from normalcy? Who am I,
staring at the others? Why are *you* staring at me? Is there a tem-
plate for suffering? Do we deserve this somehow? End of question period.

"Hon," says the receptionist, "down the hall to Dr. O'pea . . ."

In this land called Rehab (Latin: ability, aptness), I am waiting for the doctor whose name sounds like the Queen in her
Chair, Cassiopeia. That's what the constellation is called, the
kind bright queen of night, powerful and guiding. O human
configuration of stars, doctor of the five brightest stars, will
you light me into a pattern of motion, will you unscramble my
coordinates, reconstellate me to ability, return me upright to the
land of the sparkling world again? Because I need to return, to
work, to buy, to cook, to greet, to help. Meanwhile I need to
keep hold of what keeps me safe; the offices of tenderness, the
duties that I can still perform for my child. Dr. Cassiopeia, be
a constellation for healing, lean down from the sky. Will you
return me, help me keep hold, queen and healer?

I wait, you wait, we all wait.

The man over there alone waits with a swollen leg
positioned on a board that sticks straight out in front of his
wheelchair. Screws are scattered in the leg and a long thin
brace travels between them. It is as though the leg is crucified,
or is a kind of human cactus. What is this? Where am I? Muti-
lated icon or beneficiary of a "state-of-the-art" mending de-

vice, his leg grabs the attention of every patient in the waiting room. How can he bear up under the scrutiny? But at least he doesn't seem in pain.

Patient: from the Latin, to suffer, permit, allow. He has suffered, you have suffered, we have all suffered, many much more than I have.

My husband and I enter a windowless room, for yet another interrogation of the body. I strip, wondering about Fatima, wondering about the perseverance of this trauma, waiting for a stranger with an exotic name, a "caregiver" among many others who have touched my body, almost caressed it, for diagnosis, for healing that didn't, for unlocking the inchoate mystery of pain, atrophy, muscles that won't. In fact, your body becomes violatable, fair game for anyone to whom you give permission, because you have to. But the medical touch can investigate, and touch can learn, and the touch can dare too far. When you *permit* it, you can't know its true goal. So you must *suffer* it, allow it.

I look at this room, an unlovable and unloved one. There are dark frame-shaped smudges on the wall, and lighter patches of beige where pictures once hung. Picture hooks remain; there is nothing else to look at except my husband's wary, exhausted face, and the Naugahyde examining table. Why don't they take the hooks down, paint over the wall? Don't they remind you, I ask him, of meat hooks? But he can't understand: he doesn't feel like meat, not everyone feels like meat. Some of us in the Halt and Lame Club do, like flesh eaten up by pain, or portioned up, dressed with watercress and served on a platter for the doctors, administrators, petty bureaucrats.

Without knocking, Dr. Cassiopeia slices in (for she does seem compact and sharp and glinty, like a shard of something).

"So, you are an English teacher. Not so well I speak English," she announces imperiously. "So?"

So this is my queen of the sky from her throne? I flinch: against her words, against her frightening miniature perfection, I am a mess. Worse, an English teaching mess. (Lately my clothes don't fit, my large Adidases are usually untied because I can't bend over.) My toenails are long and blue, like Howard Hughes's. Her hair is perfectly cut, an uninflected white. She wears large diamond earrings (those, at least, are like stars), elegant clothes.

"So, we keep you here probably. You know you will be needing to. After I am examining you, we see." She devours my chart.

Keep me here. The words hit like steel Ping-Pong balls in my head.

Keep me here in the land of twenty-six balconies and crucified legs? The hair raises on my arms, and my blood boils. Now she seems like an elegant pistol, aimed for the heart of my life. "I can't. I need to be with my daughter." If I can't do for my child, what will happen to me? I am defined by the few physical things I can still do, like play with her on the floor, eat with her down there too, go to her school and watch the activities from the rug.

"Let's see." She glares. "Five years down. Five physical therapists. It's time to be getting you better. It is being my job to see."

I lie down. I submit to an exam. I hear her hum, and then accelerate to more of a buzz. Now she's an insect, hands flying all over my body; this body feels bitten by more exposure, another examination. She reads the chart three times, then stares, straightens her mauve washed-silk skirt. "Now I am asking your husband to leave, please now."

"I want him here." My words sound final and authoritative to me, but she is a concentrate of power. (Cassiopeia is the guide for the skies, not the dictator. The real queen would be serene, golden, pouring nurturance from a chalice, gently talking to me.)

"Privately, women must talk," she concludes. She will decide my treatment, whether I can use the hospital's facilities and therapists, so my husband and I must obey.

When he's gone, furiously gone, she says, "So how are things with your husband?" I recognize the "innocent" question from before, the question they ask before they hand out the Positions Sheet for the "crippled," for the pained. What she means is "Do you have sex?" I say nothing. Do *you* have sex, I am asking her inside my humiliation, and then, yes, she pulls the sexual guide from the drawer. Eight well-executed drawings of couples who look as graceful as the Flying Wallendas. Mild rehab porno.

How are things? my Ultimate Doctor Tyrant asks. *How are things in your house?* In ours, he cooks, does laundry, cleans, drives to the hospital and back, does all the strenuous tasks for our daughter, puts up with depression on a spree, the claustrophobic steady anger that turns us into two terriers gnawing on each other.

How about including *that* terrier position in the *Crippled Person's Guide to Sex?* You tell us sex is possible with a brief and simple rearrangement of limbs, a bit of variation and patience. But pain is not narrowly confined, leaving the rest of the willing flesh to be used luxuriously, with pleasure and verve (you should know this, Dr. Advice). It is a spreading stain, Dr. Helmet Hair, little pistol mouth, a stain through your sense of body as joy or even as adequate to the task. Try, you who knows me for half an hour and violates my sexual privacy, you little bat with Tiffany earrings, try feeling sexy with a cane by the bed, brace over the buttocks, when your shoes have to be this clumpy, frumpy kind to fit your swollen feet.

"You will be listening to me?" she says, from a great hollow distance.

This is a face-off: animals we are and always will be, adrenaline pumping up my will, saliva loose in the combative mouth. Her eyes are so close to me that I can see the bright coal in them. "To be getting you better," she states, "you must stay here in the hospital. Better to be away from work without stressing of family." I am thinking, I'm getting out of here, not anything like alive, if I stay. What do I mean? I feel imperiled, precipitous. I have counted all the jumpable balconies.

"I can't," I tell her. "It's family keeping me going. He does all the work anyway. I can't stay."

"You are meaning you won't."

"I am meaning I can't." I am going to cry.

When she leaves the room, churning up a small wind in her indignation, I sit on the examining table, a model for dejection had Rodin wanted to take on that unsensual theme. The insect has stung, the pistol has fired. I'm refusing. Maybe I won't be permitted to do rehab here unless I live here. I am quietly howling in the trap. But she is saying, Do it our way, or you can't join the Salvation Club. And the club is a last resort.

Is this club the last resort? What is the price of entry? I'm hung on the wall again; I'm hardly reconstellated in a new sky. I am back in the underground of defeat.

We go home, the winter gray subsuming the blue of April

out the window, the power lines crisscrossing like ganglia in the late afternoon. Past the hospital, down the Dantesque drive, past the mini-mall, past Star Market, where I want to be able to shop again the way some people want to go to Greece.

"Do you understand why I can't live there?" I ask my worn-out husband. I know he doesn't. Shaking with fear, I hear the other Paradox in the car, bumping along with me in the Subaru, shrouded in gauze. Paradox says, *We will take you from what keeps you sane in order to heal your troubled back. We will mend by breaking.*

When I speak back, I am not heard. *But my daughter's soothing need of me is a healing balm. See how I care for her in ways I still can. That is rehabilitation too. She does not agitate — she is manna. I need to take care of her.*

Paradox answers: *I'm sorry this does not fit with the profile on the stress chart. We know what we know about these things.* Paradox wears earrings and has smiled, has refused to see that this might be different, has labeled me in a way that Eliot has described with the "eyes that fix you in a formulated phrase."

I am repudiated again. This will be an eternal tableau: my husband driving, me back here silenced, earthbound. Dr. Cassiopeia, for a few moments that day, in the car of silent double monologue, the sky did fall with me in it, falling again, and you were the starless agent.

Massaging the base of my spine one morning, with tenderness and vigor, my physical therapist told me that there would have been no "therapeutic benefit" to my staying at the rehab. I asked her if they will ever put the pictures (Swiss Alps that can't be climbed? Wisconsin cows on inaccessible hills?) back up on the walls, or if they will ever provide stools for climbing onto the chilly, narrow examining tables.

Do they think we're gazelles? I wonder, imagining the animals leaping through these halls like dancers. "Are we supposed to leap up to the tables before we run through the veld?" I ask her.

Mantra Land

Blue meditation: from the floor I see the light blue fabric of the clearing spring sky, and think of something I read in a Peter Matthieson book about nature's rhythms: "The meeting and parting of living things is as when clouds, having come together, drift apart again, or as when leaves are parted from the trees." But I think the meeting and parting of living things is sometimes violent and ragged, especially the parting of movement and fluidity from the body. So those words are too ethereal to really mean anything, particularly to me, the woman on the floor who is scrutinizing the pure sky outside the window and remembering all the times since the injury, when she has imagined herself *not*. *Look out through the blue stained glass to a hot June day a month ago and remember lying down in a pew in order to go to a wedding: the embarrassment, the humiliation. Remember imagining the blue glass cracking, the sky beyond it cracking, the self dispersing and cracking.* A kind of blasphemy, that thought. So now, while I am supposed to be breathing out the slow sediments of disability, making my own health, if I can just find the tools, I am thinking of blue, blank blue, cracked blue, the cornflower blue of my daughter's intelligent eyes. I can't disperse and I can't crack apart.

In this Meditation Room of the rehabilitation hospital they will teach us to build new selves, to exhale the grief of our new disabilities, inhale the light of our breath, just like that. They will teach us that we must throw down the burden of our bodies, simply throw it down, this physical oppression. We are supposed to have immaculate energy that will save us, health that we simply breathe in: Salvation breathing. *Father Relaxation, Mother Meditation, deliver us, carry us on your backs to the central waters.* In my case, and in many others, push the goddamn wheelchairs. *Beget us. Make us peaceful. Pacify.*

On red plastic mats in the room we hear all the usual jargon: prioritize goals, investigate the stress you were under when the injury occurred, learn to relax fully. We look up, as Matisse's torn paper dancers mock us from the wall with their exquisite physical freedom. *O body swayed to music, O brightening glance, how can we know the dancer from the dance?* How, indeed? The dancer is the one who *can* dance. Who chooses this art for these hospitals? "You create your own health," the teacher is saying. Obediently, we will now vomit the detritus of our former lives, so that we may be full of radiant health, and pain-free. We will now choose a mantra, as commanded. Two syllables, like a healthy heartbeat. I believe in none of this, but would *like to believe* in meditation and breathing. I am filled with both longing to believe and adolescent contempt for it, so my mantra for today is *fuck you.* I'd like to take the fluffy-haired teacher, before whom I lie supplicant in my usual position, and make her suffer her own lie of responsibility for physical health, for control over the body's frailty. You with the perfect mobility, say that lie over and over to the young stroke victims whose heads wobble like toy birds, as they lose, forever, their real youth in this rehabilitation hospital. Go preach it to the Guillain-Barré people who are stricken by a virus as random as a bee sting. Out for a walk one day, they come back to become gradually paralyzed. Can they build new bodies if they only brandish enough serenity, enough good energy? Can they achieve body volition, even as their limbs drift like seaweed in the warm therapy pool?

So, a new mantra, two syllables that seem appropriate. *Dumpster, Dumpster.* That's my joke, on the floor of many floors, all the couches or lawn chairs where I have been lying for a long time, never upright except when floating in water. *Dumpster, dump her.* If this hospital gives up on me, that's where I am going to be. In the Dumpster, metaphorically speaking, in the street, in the trash. That's the way I get through the day, joking about the flat darkness, spitting out the stones: anger is my salvation, my fuel and my helium. The teacher says, Practice your mantra. Believe me, I will. We lie quietly: none of us is serene.

Desiderata

Abide with us.

Walk quietly into the room and fill yourself with the exact, uneasy presence of another person, not with a quick, empty clinical assessment of personality or stature. Fill with an energy for your patient's awaited moment, not with fatigue from thinking you have heard it all before, or the boredom you feel, the potential for frustration, even terror of the unknown. As you approach the metal table, warm your hands, because the human flesh before you is cold and terrified, and also paradoxically overheated with mystery. Your hands should seek etiological cause, or heal while gloved in warmth, not with the cool of a stranger's detachment. Linger as you speak of what you find: do not move away quickly, as though shocked or disgusted, or jaded by the persistence of frailty, the often ruined temple of the soul, troubled by fear that is a kind of exile.

Our voices are the one tremulous voice of the *patient,* the *we,* who *allow* you to see vulnerability, pain, terror, and *permit* you to hear it. Do not violate the oath: do no harm. For we are standing here suffering before you, half dressed and shivering, and we feel blown about, like twigs in the winter wind, by too much medical coldness. Coldness *is* harm: indifference to the human voice is harm; distrusting its attempt to describe difficult trouble, another harm.

Believe our voices, our quavering hands that show you where pain or disease has taken residence. Do no harm, neither with doubting eyes, nor with a voice that ices the air with remote theory, that retreats into formality and sits like a hawk above itself, a hawk in white cloth. We know you need some distance to diagnose, but fly down, believe us. For not to be believed is the child's terror and becomes the adult's humiliating secret fear. Do you sometimes negate because you have not known pain or illness to live there before? Or because the complaints do not align with anatomical diagrams?

For you are the layers-on of hands, the shamans' hands with which you will shape cure, or cause harm. Medicine begins when you walk in, begins in a confrontation that is too often seen as one between the healthy and knowledgeable, and the downcast and weak. Therefore, be gentler and display an empathy for the suffering or discomfort you see before you. State the empathy: make your words a shawl; do not just see a medical stereotype, or patient number ten of this particular exhausting day. Empathy costs nothing, steals nothing from your soul, takes no more time to summon than an instant of hostility or exhaustion or cynicism. Empathy means entering into that crowded yet cavernous space of illness, feeling the unique texture in your mind, feeling that wind blowing in the center of physical unrest or despair.

If you cannot *see* or *feel* what we tell you, then pause, and listen again to the fatigued, convinced voices of suffering, and to the spaces between the approximating words trying to describe symptoms, night sweats, dis-ease, horror. The voice is *in you* also: you will someday share in its hesitance and rambling fear, because no one escapes. (Is that what terrifies, turns some of you to ice?) Ask a question that helps to illumine, helps us to refer to another better season of the body, another climate of the healthier spirit. Try to approximate for yourself how unlit and mute is this cave of sickness, or new disability, or old depression. How odd the empty and overpopulated shape of chronic pain, or how bare the miles of living with long illness, or trouble, or accident.

If you cannot understand, say, *I cannot understand.* Do not turn away in ignorance or humiliation because of your failed knowledge or your challenged status. Do not turn your unknowing back on the patients, blaming them for presenting you with mystery, or with a labyrinth of suffering with no apparent way out.

Look at the person before you. Acknowledge the struggle to be endured. Say, *There is a struggle. It must be difficult. I am sorry, your life so changed, your family upset.* Say, I feel for you, and know your own potential struggle as a frail organism. (There is sickness, new sickness, a scorching virus, and more forms of violence than ever seen before.)

Speak with words that are given like food, even if the food is strange. Put nutrition in them, acknowledge with them your patient's hunger for surcease, and for comfort. (Some of you know this. Feed us.) If there is the clinical sheath on the words, unsheathe them and show an understandable truth; do not highlight the difference in status between well and sick with an armory of expertise and expert metallic words of detachment.

Sit side by side and talk, even if you do not know precisely what is ruining or failing or hurting this substantial mother-born person before you. Side by side: not behind the barrier of your protecting desk. The desk is not a moat.

Offer continuity when the appointment is over, even as you send us off to the lab for diagnostic detective work, send us home, send us to rehabilitation, to the pharmacy, to nothing at all, promise you will be a temporary axis for this particular frightening world. The person who has become a patient is without a clear map in many ways, indeed lost inside the planet of the once familiar body: being lost, without compass, without steadying axis, also terrifies adults as much as children. There is a need for directions, a night-light, for an immense darkness falls over the body in claustrophobic fear of itself. The body in health does not notice itself: sick, it glares at us. Acknowledge that possible lostness in yourself, that glare which is only a shadow of what we feel as we enter.

*

Now imagine yourself before us. We speak to you slightly: you are half dressed, in deplorable confusion. We do no technical harm, we don't blink or talk or even notice the color of your eyes. Step up to this table. *Tell us the problem. Point to it. No, the table is not cold. No one else complains about it. That can't be: pain there means something else. I'm not going to belabor the point. You should be progressing. The drugs should be working. Are you taking them? Go home. Go to the hospital. Come back and see me. Try to have a better attitude.* (We tell you everything *we* have heard.) *Be clearer. Get dressed. Come in the other room. The human sufferer is an unreliable narrator,* we say to you. Our hands are all over you, seeking, not finding, poking.

You turn around. Your shoulders, you say, are cold. It's cold in the room. Your hands, you say, are always cold and blue. We do not reach out to feel them, we know blue is only relative.

We have the power to say: *Sorry, can't find much. Or, More tests? Can you stand that? Or, This has been going on for a long time, it must exhaust you, you must feel uncomfortable.* But we don't. We button our coats, clutch our folders. Your tears, welling indiscreetly in your eyes, make us feel closer to the exact address of emptiness where we might weep. And your fear, your oxygen-eating fear, amplifies ours. But we have power. You have none at the moment.

*

Now we become patients again.

We say to you, With so much power, walk carefully and humbly. Do no harm: walk carefully so that the granite weight of that power does not crush. Abide with us.

Pools

CHILD BRIEFLY UNDER

Four or five years old: they are all crazy in the water, with their
swerving floats and puffy swim cuffs. My daughter gleams
brightly out there; her whitish hair is so beautiful, it makes me
nervous for her. Is it so conspicuous that it will be a liability
later? And she's too cheerful, and compliant, with all the abrupt
changes, adaptations, and uncommon disappointments that Pain
the Dictator causes. (At the last minute, pain and its hangers-
on have today decided to vacate, so we can go swimming at
this large pool in the suburbs.) Someone owns a big house and a
big pool, and this is strange and wonderful to her; she questions
why people need to have a lot of space, big anything, when
small and cozy will do. (Couldn't we live, she said, dipping her
toes into socialism, as she dips them into the turquoise water,
with M., who had recently purchased an enormous house.) She
swims well.

There are many children here, kicking and careless and chaotic, the kind of scene to send the purposely childless person over the edge — disorder, silly-looking floats shaped like lobsters, dinosaurs, flowers, hot dogs; parents who look distracted; sloppy tables with orange soda and chips spilled together to make a kind of picnic gravy so often present at gatherings with young children. For the moment, I am sitting here, assessing the stairs down to the water. On the edge, and directly on the other side of the pool steps from me, is a woman. We are equidistant from each other and from the clutch of children ramming their floats in the shallow end about three feet from the steps. This is very important, the equidistance, for it will be the word that snags me for years like a hook. We are talking well, equidistant from each other and the children; she is a woman of humor and complexity. (Usually these gatherings are avoided: people do not know how to approach a lying-down woman, and worse, seem *unable* to leave — pity? guilt? — so we get stuck in "disability glue" — I not wanting them to stay, and they, who do not want to stay either, but seem to give themselves no choice.) Intently, we watch how surprisingly strong the children are, how little they practice what they know about water safety, how well they love the splashy zing and jazz of water, the high jinks, the mischievous trick of turning the floats fast, jamming them, just like in the cars at the fair. My daughter is on a crocodile float, too long for her, I later realize; too big for a small, thin child, competent in water but not a complete swimmer yet, not with the necessary confidence.

"She's under, she's under," someone shouts, and simultaneously I see, know, and try to move fast, fast, adrenaline shot through me like voltage. I am vibrating with panic, but some-

one else has her: *I can't move fast enough to rescue my own child.*
Thank God, she's fine, scared and fine. Equidistant, equidistant. She's safe.

Much later, after my own brand of reproof and self-repudiation, after the spreading knowledge of this ultimate failure, the insult to my own particular motherhood, the word *mortified* found a place in my vocabulary. And then fury turned toward those others who had said disbelievingly all those years, "Oh, you could run if you *had* to. If there was a fire or accident, you'd move faster than you think you can." Oh, yes?

She was under: this overly contemplated moment is now like a punishing home movie, played over and over. Why do I half remember that woman trying to make my daughter think it was me, the woman becoming an embodiment of compassion, caring. How did she do it, let go, then shove the float over to me? Was it an illusion?

But child, I couldn't get there faster than the other person; you are mine, and I failed. You're safe and that's the heart of everything. (But I — applying the relentless solipsism that accompanies crisis, or averted crisis, as it is influenced by physical difference — I failed.) If I had been there alone, you probably would have been all right, probably; but there were other adults around. Another woman beat me to my own child, a five-year-old facedown, flipped under a float in the water.

Summertime, horizontal time, no patterns, just accident and averted accident. She was not the mother. My child was safe, she is fine. I was the mother goddess fallen, a mother manqué. Motherhood was orphaned for a minute, the absence of body volition confirmed; and years later, I still ache with gratitude for that woman, nameless and generous in her deliverance.

Oh, we are such good parents, such educated Penelope Leach parents, enlightened and determined to redress the confusing opacity of our childhoods, where mysterious events went unexplained, and we were left bewildered. *Don't you think,* I said, *she should see with her own eyes where her mother is all day, so she won't be worried and think I'm secretly at some cancer hospital, or where everyone is terminally ill?* We are progressive nursery school parents, we could be the subject of satire, so close to the stereotypical kind of liberal parents we are: we need four hands to calculate her welfare, her comfort, her desires, and we have not enough arms to hug, to arrange, to buy. We should be a parent made of octopus arms, not two people.

But we are companions and mates whose lives have undergone massive change: hook, line, sinker, the whole shebang, the whole basket with all the broken eggs. When I was first injured, she began watching the new reel unwind, with me in the emergency room, with her omnipotent mother (hyperactive, always useful) too weak to stand, then on the bed, on the floor. Her mother became too strange an animal, stiff and unable to lift her, an unknown, as unpredictable as life inside the house itself had become, with strangers in and out, and physical therapists now touching the body that was previously all hers to climb, to be with, to be carried by. She grew jealous of them. And now she is four; her parents spend arduous hours guessing about the cumulative adverse effects on her, trying to cushion other blows, more usual disappointments, trying to manage house, hearth, and heart coherently and with a degree of joy and stability.

And so, with much good intent, we decide to take her to the rehabilitation hospital, especially to the pool for hydro-therapy because — we guess, oh, we think we are *right* — she'll love the huge oversized floats, and all the physical thera-pists who look like Olympic swimmers in their identical tank suits. She'll see where her mother goes every morning, how warm it is, how comforting.

She stares. It is unlike any other pool because it is so hot in the room, unlike any other pool because there are so many people she's never met before being pushed in those floats by the standing people in the black tank suits. And the color of the water: unreal, the color of blue plastic toys. In the floats are the damaged, wounded people, a few I had hoped wouldn't be there. (Please do not come today, paraplegics, OK? I don't want her to be scared. And by the way, keep the young stroke victims out too.)

I explain, "That's what I use, those floats, aren't they just great? I will get better here, for sure. Isn't this nice?" My daughter's face, always weighing the possibilities, always watchful, does not register the relief we expected and had tried to create: at that moment, was it a look of some trust violated, some disguised terror? We tried to remember later. On the way back we dutifully talked. We reflectively listened for her very few comments, just as we had learned from Ginott, Carl Rogers, Leach.

Later, for two or three months, she lapsed from exuber-ance, from the nonstop *joie de vivre* that was companion to her vigilance, became closed like a pod, silent and unable to tell anyone what was wrong. Wildly we guessed. What had grabbed her with terror: was the whole spectacle of a "new mother" now just catching up? Had the family imbalance —

me down, her father up, with no equality in work or physical child care — finally knocked her off *her* balance? She had the words, had *had* them young and eloquently. Whatever it was, it couldn't be spoken, out loud, though I'm sure she heard it like a troubling chorus every day. Could not be spoken to us because we were the subject of the complex web of magical thinking that can trap a child. Finally she confided to her teacher that I would fall out of those floats someday, wouldn't I? (They are so big, I had told her, so that they can hold the body completely.) And drown and die, she told her amazed and loving teacher. Go under in the warm turquoise pool.

We thought we were the most careful parents.

*

But how could we be, all the time every time? Especially, how could I be, having broken the eleventh parental commandment, Thou Shalt Provide Stability, and its subcommandment, Be as Much the Same Day by Day as You Can Be, to afford the steady unflickering presence of mother in a child's life, motherhood compleat. I became new. Was I frightening?

But we thought we were the most considerate parents, trying to anticipate fear, ambush anxiety before it became fullblown and ambushed our child. We imagined her more vulnerable because our house was so burdened with crises and the need for adaptation; our domestic mood drastically split between Before Injury, After Injury, mother upright, then mother fallen. With more plans gone askew, the world had gone just plain strange and sad suddenly. Some children go to see their mothers' workplaces: she had to see where I go for repair, the body shop, so to speak, and ended up with a fear so large it couldn't be spoken. So much for consideration, a plan for parental kindness and preparation.

And what about the spirit of the child, so well shaped and glowing at the glowing start before injury? When the living matrix of domestic life is day-to-day coping with practical matters, and smoothing over for the illusion of calm, I believe some children suffer in awestruck quiet, and then in slow, adaptive turbulence or avoidance. She saw her mother down on the pavement: after that she would never be lifted or *held* exactly the same way. For her the image must have burned deep — suddenly to be hugged by someone prone. And how loud in her mind the domestic discord in the wake? Often the pat guidance books cannot help with these issues because they prettify what is essentially awful and often visually up-setting — all set against the background atonal noise of chronic pain, and mood swings conducted by the rude baton of that pain.

All of it *was* upsetting to the eye. Even though one book said, "Children and family members must be careful to put aside feel-ings of embarrassment," how can the young child not feel odd when her parent, the only parent so placed, watches the class play from a gym mat on the shiny floor, having been lifted up four flights of stairs to the gym by her father and a friend? Lies on the floor for her haircuts, on dirty airplane floors now when they travel a little, and worst, at toy stores? Children should not be *shoulded* into denying the natural, almost tribal, desire to have a family that fits in with other families, to *not* be conspicu-ous, with a family configuration that conforms easily. And to see the parent static, not working, seemingly *not useful:* While the same book says that "both the parent and children must recognize that the burden of the workload must be shifted," how can a perceptive child not notice the parent trying to hide her sense of disempowerment under busy, nattering cheer and busier art projects? In our house, there was no manageable workload for me, except the emotional and the social planning role. (Some thought this a desirable thing, not knowing how the removal of choice hurts like a surgical cut.) To watch the fearsome removal of major responsibilities is another burden for the "adapting" child. And although any child can be made to feel important and involved in small household chores, these feelings of significance have to coexist with trauma, and the perpetual tilt of the child's terrain. And I was not going to let work shift to a small child. (The eleventh commandment falls away, and cracks in two like Moses' real stone.)

What could we do? Many of us, back in that pool in the hospital on the hill, reflecting on crises in the brilliant tropical water that reflected us back, would have liked to relinquish some worries, rather than being riven with sorrow over our imagined failure of responsibility, or the deprivation we were certain we were offering our children. We became like Rilke's panther, pacing the cage of each individual problem, with the coldest iron bars seeming to separate us from them. And like Rilke's panther, our wills "stunned and numbed" by our new emotional and physical losses, some saw "a world made of bars, a thousand bars, and behind the bars, nothing." With nothing we could do well either, or so we thought at first.

Surely being still, being comforted by the self-forgiving notion of an A for effort, would have been better than rattling the bars in anger, than noisily clinking the ice in the glass, or the rushes of drugs or irritability, and a serious dive into despair, and worse. Could some of us never enter the peace of partial adjustment because of self-recrimination, despite proffered help? In my case, despite my overworked, underpraised husband; despite a supportive mother who visited so often, and helpful friends, still I woke in the night alone, feeling doomed to being a horizontal and less useful parent. Some were already in traction or bed or wheelchair and feared for the self's survival, and for the ability of their worlds to remain coherent, especially for their children. All of us feared for our children's fine receptive minds, inscribed on a daily basis with *our* new depression, and *their* ever sharper discomfort, in spite of our laborious attempts to cover up both in cheer so thin it could break like twigs in winter. (Who could hide the anguish of not protecting a child that day in the pool?) And no well-intentioned articles on children and disabled parenthood could help, no comments on troubled parenthood, on mentally ill parents, parents of every "different" type imaginable, did any good either because it is always the one absolutely unique B-flat music of daily life in a "differently" upset household that damages the one uniquely tuned-in child. Despite all the abundant overcompensating love, the damage too arises from the parent's elemental guilt so large that indeed the least sound in the child's psyche makes for real trembling in the parent: guilt about taking her to the pool, guilt about being in the therapeutic pool instead of at home, guilt about being in irascible pain when not in the pool.

Later I waited for her fear of my early "drowning" to resurface, and awaken again the dozing guilt about my overly conscientious mistake. But guilt be damned, even though I still see those turquoise pools wink at me like senseless neon signs.

What can we all say, we panthers, or children of angry, guilty panthers? We can say that the road to rehabilitation is paved with gentle, grossly mistaken good intentions to repair what can't be repaired exactly, or rebuilt. And that it is not paved with gold or emeralds, but everywhere strewn with the pages of throwaway guidance books — and down that road go changed families, changed friendships, changed selves.

Angels of Attempted Repair

In the warm milky pool, people are coupling and uncoupling in the water. Pressed together in every mix of gender, they look like water animals never before seen, many-limbed and two-headed. For this aquatherapy many of us are in large yellow floats, our legs wrapped under the strong muscular arms of the physical therapists: our angels of attempted repair. We lie back, supplicant, and they exercise our arms. Our feet rest near their breasts or on their bellies, where we push off, then back, push off, then release, to move our unwilling legs. Viewed from above, this could look like a strange water bacchanal with everyone contorted, everyone intimate.

The angels are dressed in their Sporto tanks, faded to bronze but formerly black. We wear our oldest suits, some from the sixties with loud, Beatles colors, because the water bleaches out the fabric. (The chlorine is almost unbearably high because some people are incontinent.) Some of us in this water have an excess of sensation, like a bad distillate, which is pain, from the Latin, *poena*, for payment or penalty. Others being swirled around have too little sensation, a "goneness" in their bodies that is paralysis, and they need the pool therapy so muscles won't atrophy. The water soothes and blesses us: like water astronauts in floats, we have descended down the stairs into the near bliss of weightlessness. For a while the joints and the spine do not jackhammer the body, or chatter away with their shrill messages. And the hands of the angels try to transport us, their bulky cargo, from one body-state across the border of water to a better one — surcease. Sometimes they fail, but they are practical and optimistic so they try again.

We have fallen from grace and we know why empirically: injury, illness, strange viruses that shut down the nerves. But not *Why* . . . In the hospital, you see the idea of randomness made flesh: the one event that goes like a heave of lightning into a life, rending it from that too bright moment on. But we no longer ask that Why: Why the penalty, why the punishment? However, if you could take all the now-quieted energy in this pool and convert it into electricity, we could light up Boston and Hong Kong. We could be a new source of unnatural power.

Sometimes we can accommodate pain, as we would accommodate an intractable relative, or a tenant who won't get out. Its vivid presence lives in us as love would, if it ever came back. We feel unmanned and unwomaned by what has happened; for some of us sexual love has fled, even affection has disappeared, for the chronic relentless *thereness* of pain creates an anger that makes others unwilling to offer caresses. And sometimes any touch can produce pain. Our bodies are the thieves of pleasure, and we have no confidence this will ever change.

But we do not complain to the angels; they are here to work us, to make us flexible and even functional. But it is ironic how we are forced unprotesting into these positions of sexual intimacy, when in this blue other-world there is probably less activity, and more urgency to retrieve it, than in any other pool for hundreds of miles. But we never tell the angels this because they are not for mulling over sadness. Instead, we swear a lot in the pool, we laugh our lunatic fun-house laughter, though we are bewildered and bitter.

As we float and bend and exercise, we make horrible jokes about "crips," about the silly "well-meaning" things people say. ("I wish *I* could stay in bed for a month. I'd catch up on my reading.") Mostly, there is incessant talk about food, hosannas of praise for chocolate, for pie, for steaks, all discussed in delicious detail. The angels tell us it is always so. Through the years each group in the pool rhapsodizes and argues about recipes, about intricate variances in preparation, about ethnic dishes and restaurants; counts calories; compares diets; debates the merits of Bertucci's pizza versus Mario's, until someone will shout "Stop!" But no one can, and everyone in the pool keeps spinning the long, loving exuberant tale of food. It is the oral history of the rehabilitation hospital. It is what does *not* betray, what gratifies, fills, grants a multiplicity of caresses to the mouth, kisses to the taste buds. Sometimes people will talk of the last meal before the accident, the last meal sitting in an upholstered chair, not a wheelchair, everything described with painterly obsession about texture and color: pancakes, lasagna, chicken gumbo, doughnuts dipped in cocoa powder. We look up at the damp ceilings and paint visions of food there, and our appetite builds on the rising wave of our passionate talk. We can smell cooking fragrances. Pain, which does not sit still in one part of the body, has not destroyed this pleasure. Pain is a moving army, but food resists it. And as we engage in the pseudo-Kama Sutra of physical therapy, the rounded memories of eating fill us like desire, and the angels know this. Our hunger for our lost bodies is here in the talking, the languorous talking.

Over there in the corner by the wall an angel stands upright, wrapping a young man's legs around her hips. When she lets go, his limbs drift loosely, so she wraps them around her again. He looks ecstatic, and sated as he lies back, and they seem as tightly woven together as in inventive lovemaking. In fact, he is recently paralyzed and she is exercising him — she *does* to him, to his limbs, they do not do for each other — because the control of his muscles has fled. In the guise of intimate positioning, this healing posture prevents him from worsening. Comfort and help, but no joy.

When they are through, when the angel decides the exercises are over, she puts him very carefully into a canvas seat and harness (if his head rolls down to touch the water, he could drown) and hoists him out with a small powerful crane. He ascends into gravity again, later into the wheelchair that goes into the shower, then back to his hospital room. I notice the staff has forgotten to give him long bathing trunks, and his taped catheter and urine bag show. I know by his downcast face that he knows, and he can't move his arms to cover them. He must feel even more abject — if it is possible — with this new visible mark of humiliation.

We are happy in the water, 98.6 degrees, the temperature of coveted normalcy, and we hate to leave. On the ground gravity presses on our joints and our spines like a spreading vise. We levitate in the pool, we can go places with a special waist belt. Side to side, traveling what seems like acres in our belts that let us walk almost weightlessly, we escape the small rooms of ourselves, and the way the body has become a cage that seems to exist only for trapping the self inside. Beneath talking and beyond sharing it, pain is what the angels help us bear. Walking in this water we have the illusion of power and freedom, like flying.

In fact, the absence of pain has become one definition of the sensual. For a while in the soothe of water, I am not afraid of what will hurt next, what seismic tremor will hit me or how many days I will have to lie flat. I want nothing but more luxurious talk of food, my limbs to be exercised gently and swirled around as weightlessly as foam, as my physical therapist guides the muscles. It is enough for me. For some of us in the pool, it is the most gratifying part of the day: a colorful apex in a mostly flattened landscape . . .

Until we have to get out, and then it begins, the yearning for walking unbrokenly or with ease. Gravity assumes its pull as we hit the blue-tiled stairs and floor; wanting assumes its pull. Imagine us, waiting to walk painlessly with an almost erotic longing — for me a wait of three years, for others much longer. Like waiting for Eros, it has the sweet presence of anticipation, an almost tactile buildup; and then someday, perhaps the event itself will occur, the high epiphany of Walking, the luxury and the goal itself. Two shoes, two legs that cooperate with each other and with the spine, traversing the complex earth without canes or walkers, moving across the terrain according to natural command from the nervous system, hips not protesting but agreeing to motion; then to catch finally the gold ring of walking, then joy, satiety . . . all this far off, but deeply imagined and felt. Relief at gravity the companion again, not the enemy, the body dilating with joy in the sensual idea of motion. I can see myself walking around my own block someday, or even farther off, and maybe always impossible, the cobblestones of an exotic city.

I can't do it yet. But in this pool, with the small ripples of human exercise and effort circling around me, I have walked many miles over three years in my blue world-traveling magic belt. My angel has pushed me, yelled at me, comforted and cooed at me, still getting impatient with my fear of my body, bullying me to have some hope. Sometimes I hate her, but then I think of walking on land, how difficult, and I work harder; I think of walking around Florence perhaps, with the sienna light falling around the city and over the Arno near dusk.

It's a misty day, or perhaps a harsh day in winter. Or spring, and the earth is breathing out green, with banners of wind all around. I am walking toward a person I haven't yet met, a *you* that is not in my life now. The substantial tasteable pleasure you have to give makes me walk faster toward you, though of course I can never run. I hear the serious ringing of the Duomo bells, and the joy in my body from walking on my own two legs like this exceeds even what I anticipate in miles of pleasure from you.

And then on the other side of the pool, I hear a new recipe for lasagna from Gloria S., who traveled here from North Carolina to visit family and got the Guillain-Barré virus one day in Dorchester and has been paralyzed ever since. She knows what random is. "Repeat that please," I say. "How can you *not* cook the noodles? Do you have a recipe for corn pudding?"

"How about concentrating on this exercise?" my angel says, lifting me and sailing me around her sturdy hips in the water.

Gratitude / Chiaroscuro

> Do not think I am not grateful for your small
> kindness to me.
> I like small kindnesses.
> In fact I actually prefer them to the more
> substantial kindness, that is always eying you,
> like a large animal on a rug,
> until your whole life reduces
> to nothing but waking up morning after morning
> cramped, and the bright sun shining on its tusks.
>
> — *"Gratitude," Louise Glück*

ONE

She is on the floor, hungry, and can't get up because of pain, really hungry and vocal about it, though patient. The house is frenetic: sick cat, children running, phones jarring, arrangements for car repair, and just one person to do all of it. It's winter and the floor is cold, though blankets for comfort and warmth have been placed — by him, naturally — over and under the worn exercise mat.

Then he hands her a white paper plate with a bright boiled hot dog stranded between two slices of white bread. It is food (shouldn't she be happy for that?), but it is disgusting to her: unadorned, fat and pink like some vestigial food organ, or a joke from the same store that sells plastic vomit. *That* she doesn't mention. Here's what she knows: she's supposed to feel grateful. Someone brought food to someone who couldn't get food: human to human, an act of kindness, appeasement, and generosity, all of which the world is known to badly need, to put it mildly.

Gratitude is expected, but no, this one on the floor, this *I* surveyed as *she,* feels like a dog that has been fed and must then lift moist eyes upward in thanks to its owner — the purveyor of food, the giver of small and large continual incessant kindnesses — must repress revulsion at the Dickensian meal. Of course he has more than enough on *his* plate, is doing almost everything in the whole honeycombed complexity of a household, is too tired to think of choice, or mustard, or toasted bun or china plate. But it's as though food has been thrown to me: I can't complain, must try to feel always always always, gratitude for the big beast of steady kindnesses which has come to the door.

Gratitude, *scuro,* dark: no other concept can seem so rigid and uncomfortable when forced, when not felt but pretended. So I shut up. I thank. I eat the aerated off-white bread, and so it is, a typical weekend in the mess of adjustment, with the insincere, barely uttered thanks barely noticed in the cacophony of disorganization, with his internal monologues probably raging too: *Got the lunch ready, didn't I, and the food shopping done and the weights for your exercises bought and the rug vacuumed.* Easy for him to protest, wearing the protective mask of kindness over his molten anger. Easy for him to walk away to work, to run, to pick up his child: he doesn't have to lie here in a whirlpool of physical change and self-pity and a feeling of helplessness. He doesn't have to feel grateful every minute of every day. And on and on: the script of many households in sudden disruptive change.

And so a certain kind of bastardized gratitude becomes the currency of dependency. Upon receiving both "favors" and necessities, it is expected. To keep peace, one must *act* grateful: the etiquette is as carefully laid out as in the old Emily Post. Gratitude is the good behavior extracted from the recipient of multiple kindnesses: a form of bitter payment between adults, who — while honorable and fair-minded — are trapped. As time goes on, giving gratitude becomes a labor in itself, when one person is always *doing* and the other receiving. It stinks like old broccoli. As years of "unableness" continue, gratitude makes the relationship between donor and recipient a briar patch. Soon the whole house is filled with one person's extreme gratitude, gratitude in every corner, until all that is given stands, with tusks center stage and shining, demanding *notice, notice*, see how grateful you should be.

The cosmic issue is that the previously autonomous person *would like to reciprocate,* would like to perform all those "kindnesses" for her/himself. I wanted to select my own clothes, drive myself, buy my own clothes, buy my own canes, my own presents for others; I couldn't. So sometimes the real wish was to say in moments of excruciating bathos: *Take me out and shoot me or leave me by the side of the road,* instead of, *Thank you, thank you, thank you again.* Unless a couple is sophisticated in the convoluted art of tactful tending, beyond any usual earthling capacities, the negotiation of acts of daily care takes over, gobbles affections, equilibrium, and harmony. Though no one is ever at fault, I know it is harder for the recipient — who should feel unpinched gratitude and doesn't, and becomes knotted with subsequent guilt. There's no choice, *in extremis:* one needs the huge beastlike kindness.

Of course, at some time most people experience some dependence, some large or smaller need, and then spontaneous untainted gratitude is easily felt — a gift of gratitude for a gift of satisfying a temporary, finite want or a need. But when help is ongoing and for subsistence, and a paradigm of exchange is set up, the resultant self-renewing outrage at dependence tyrannizes individual personality and the personality of the couple in turn. This diminishes the space where the couple lives, as though there were now three domestic forces, man, woman, and gratitude — hers. While *not* demanded, I suspect there's a secret expectation of thanks on the part of all overworked unpaid caregivers, in order to keep going, from *Thank me for what I have done for you,* to the mostly unvoiced, more serious *Many others would not do this,* and the penultimate, furious *Others I know would have left by now.* The weather is dangerous in such a cramped space.

But within that weather, I, the currently not horizontal woman, would say also penultimately, I *am* purely grateful now, even with the wretched hot dog still on a plate in my mind. I am now, but when did it ever stop then? There was little to make others feel grateful to me, and no end to the servitude to thankfulness. How do you get up from the pose of gratitude — on your knees? To have been so helped: Yes, I perfectly know many would have left. I can now do for myself, but when I couldn't, my thanking was stingy and dark, and my anger was too bright and fed on the dark.

TWO

Chiaro, light: the well-lit face of the other gratitude surfaces from the *freedom* to give it, and is always given beneficently. For me this kind was felt most intensely when the strong magical hands of physical therapists took pain away, however briefly. True, there is an exchange: there is consumer and formal provider of services, and healing is both the goal and (one hopes) the purchased product. All this is the tidy business part. Also true is that the professional touch — in exercises, massage, application of heat and electrical stimulation, aquacise, wax baths, helping the patient stretch with weights — is engaged in a type of wordless negotiation with the patient. But no endless demand for appreciation oils the deal. Of course, in domestic life, the new inequality of partners creates messy needs and unclear roles, and the relationship in physical therapy usually has crisp clean borders. It is not a matrix for dependence, nor ready-made for conflict. And so the gratitude that flows from the exchange is gentle, unsullied.

In the long-term, frequent physical therapy, there is the obvious retraining of the body, teaching new undestructive ways of moving, and education in general about injury and prevention. Beyond this, what is the gift? Touch first, and touch foremost, which Montague calls the mother of the senses, the most important of organ systems and the earliest to develop embryonically. The adult body in pain requires touch, having often been isolated from the mother of senses by fear; or sometimes excluded from it by worn-out mates, lovers, and children who are afraid of inflicting more damage. Often in extreme "skin hunger," many people with acquired disability or injury know too well the cold medical touch of advanced examining machines, but often they are despairingly estranged from contact with skin the longer everything goes on and feel famished.

Touch gives some vestige of kinship to ourselves. Because it helps to repair the broken or damaged part, touch rejoins the patient to the rest of the body and to the forgotten world of elemental sensuality or sensory appreciation. It sets up a kind of Morse code, as Helen Colton calls it in *The Gift of Touch*, sparking "a volt of electricity that shoots through a neuron," and, "As the electrical charge goes through, it stimulates a chemical neurotransmitter, which sparks across that synapse and ignites another electrical impulse through the next neuron . . ."

This igniting code, I believe, helps to give back the perceived map of the body, our proprioception, in which "We feel our bodies as proper to us, as our property, as our own," as Oliver Sacks has written. Called a sixth sense, proprioception tells us where things feel physically located, but this felt body knowledge is sometimes lost after injury. After so much lying down often I could not figure out how to perform simple motions, like climbing up to a therapy table, or bending to the left or right. Which foot first for stairs, and which was next, and which moved first in bending, the shoulder or waist? And where was that shoulder-in-relationship-to-arm that moves the whole act of sitting up? After much locating touch and grounding physical therapy, I began to rejoin my body, relating smoothly and unconsciously to its parts. *Chiaro:* the gratitude for this will never be in language, as the body began to find itself again coherent and awash in possibility.

There is also a sense of sanctuary in being guided by a helper on an often terrible journey. For most long-term patients, the journey is very hard, for who can bear smilingly the loss of any function? Along with that protection, often goes wonder. Among ice packs and braces and Velcro and ugly corsets and appliances and canes and walking bars on the journey, there can be a sense of awe — glittering awe in the midst of the gray monotony of painful struggle. When I first walked from the dingy entrance of the hospital to the therapy booths, I was stricken, almost prayerful. And when that withdrawn child at the hospital gets up after playing for months with a huge exercise ball and a small, lean persevering physical therapist, it is miraculous to watch the child start walking one day, as miraculous as any other resurrection. Can what the family feels be called gratitude, or is it more like ecstasy?

Do they feel a sense of deliverance? Is it almost like love, so passionate in intensity, like the emotion that men during war feel for nurses, or what women briefly, truly experience for those who deliver their babies? In fact, physical therapists are like midwives. When I was finally given a new well-being, and a functional self, I was overcome with thanks commingled with reverence. It is not surprising that we use religious language to express these emotions. As a society, we have elevated doctors to the status of demigods and we expect divine acts. But physical therapy hasn't been praised enough as a healing profession. Those workers toil in the fields of the body, doing the real labor in daily or weekly contact with muscle, joint, bone. Vigilant, they live *with* patients, lead us out when possible, and become like earthly angels of attempted repair. Tragically, because of limited visits in managed care, these angels are now less frequently available, to the detriment of everyone. And, as opposed to the all too noisy domestic fracas of upset in a family, physical therapy is quiet: the curtained booth where it happens becomes like a draped confessional where the body reveals its convoluted secrets. How can we not feel happiness for the quiet? For the angels who deliver that too?

One physical therapy manual dictates, "Be understanding but not personal with patients," along with the mundane "Wear deodorant." You, my whole therapist made of six people, to whom I owe my soul for the return of mobility, and the vanquishing of pain, are told not to be personal with me. But in your extremely focused hands and diagnosing minds, I feel the most personal gift bestowed on me: relief, homeostasis, my life recaptured, free from supplicating dependence. *The hands that, soothing, heal the pain away: the pain that, loving me, would not release and go away. The healing hands that "love" the pain away.* The urge to be personal in giving back to you is immense. What can be offered but a kind of earthly platonic gratitude, lighting up the cave?

Closed in a booth, nestled in the water for aquacise, on a plinth for home visits, we are closely attached like intimates, but without the autobiographical secret-sharing or sensual touch. The body is draped, but the whole skin of self exposed: the damaged selfhood that accompanies physical damage is being touched. Vertebra by vertebra, the hands press, squeeze, trail like silk down the spine, push their soft erudition to the target, the sacrum. The relief is spiritual, in the self of the body. Hand to skin, healer to the being healed, work and pleasure alone on a quest: this is an experience of intense closeness, despite boundaries, a closeness almost erotic but not, almost intimate but not exactly — quirkily indefinable, just as the response to being delivered is. In the same handbook, there is the unreasonable edict: "Do not accept gifts from patients," but how would anyone refuse the psychological gift of gratitude from us that is light, not heavy to give.

And sometimes, mostly when sleepless, I would wonder whether this gratitude edged too close to erotic love, so passionate it was, to a yearning beyond the need for pain and depression from it to cease. Do others wonder about this too? All but one therapist were female: Was I being imprinted with a longing for women that exceeded the longing for healing, because they saved me? I could walk and sit up in my life again because of their holy intervention: Were longing and gratitude moving like watercolors in a wash, blurring together in surprising new color?

My marriage had been under siege, seemed almost torn. Late at night, staring into what still promised to be a lastingly difficult ordeal, I would shock myself by dreaming of running away, being helped away by the physical therapist, leaving all, lock, stock, barrel, conflict, chair, and cane behind, all but my daughter. Live with your physical therapist: that's one way to hasten recovery, start anew, abandon old habits, and have a new vision. My life was beginning to return, was being resuscitated. No wonder that such gratitude could not be one color, then, and was a mix of many intensities and hues.

But here is my offering: without the work of twelve hands, hands like composite eyes working together for sight, in order for muscles and joints to *feel* and *know* how to move again, horizontal would still be horizontal. And the living out of gratitude would have been dark and cramped, like the rooms where we lived.

Drinking Jack Daniel's with
Mr. Rogers: A Retrospective

"I . . . [am] drunk

with my prime whiskey: rage."

— from "Love Song: I and Thou," Alan Dugan

At this moment, millions of women, children, men, whole day
care centers, villages, and kibbutzim, are shut in — dustbound,
homebound, or snowbound — in the blue fog of TV, watching
Mr. Rogers sing out his relentless goodness. They must be
drinking something — comfrey tea, Postum, kaffir, mead, near
beer, Dr. Pepper, and in my case, anything to warm the blue
silence outside with a warm partaking inside. I drink Jack
Daniel's and watch Fred, as I call him, for Mr. Rogers and I
have been living together these horizontal years.

Fred signals the end of another day for us, and the beginning of Jack Time, communion time without the wafer. "It's

such a good feeling to know you're alive, it's such a happy feeling," he sings every cold afternoon, shadowy afternoons that hold no mystery, the shut-in winter years. In a blizzard, there is a sense of communality; but unlike others, I don't get up and walk into it afterward for fun or beauty. In fact, the isolation without reprieve is more like being on an ice floe, with friends and relatives waving good-bye to the lying-down woman who is floating away, or that is how it is imagined. "O world of white, first home of dreams," writes the poet Howard Nemerov of a snow globe, but the beauty of snow recedes and home is no longer dreamed as good. Winter has become wintering over with Jack and Fred.

The sky outside the glazed windows is sometimes elephant-colored (like surface depression, coating the skull) and sometimes a deep vacant blue (a black and blue wordless anguish). The wolf's at the door, the world is stopped on its axis, school's closed, roads are treacherous and icy. We're trapped upstairs because there's no chair elevator yet. For the child, food is up here, juice boxes, but no ice for the Jack unless I grab a raggy icicle outside the window, while artificially sweetened Mr. Fred is telling me: *I hope that you'll remember, even when you are feeling blue, that it's you I like and everybody, every day should feel good, and it's the inside not the outside that counts.* That lost able-bodied part — the outside — shouldn't count. It does when you cease to be able-bodied. In this room there is the bedraggled ambience of an old bed-sitter, the analogue a perfectly fitting one for me. When I'm feeling blue, I should remember Fred's juicy smile, his sugary admonitions. *(Whiskey rage, oh silent night of world of white.)* Will I drown in his lying cheer and goodness, like some awful honey I am stuck in every afternoon for my child's pleasure? His sweatery warmth and Buddhistic U.P.R. (unconditional positive regard) — and the damn whistling trolley to the Land of Make-Believe — are of course what my baffled child loves, cuddled in front of the reliable TV: the perfectly composed adult who never yells; the train that goes to an imaginary place each day, when she hardly travels at all anymore; the environment never barbed with arguments or tears or whispers, or peppered with protest; the clear optimism and cheer; the sweet hokey figures who sing sweet didactic operas. *Q: What makes you cry, Mr. Knife and Fork? A: I want my spoon, my spoon,* answers the pining man dressed up as cutlery. So give him the spoon, scriptwriters. In the land of Fred, help is offered quickly, accepted graciously, and no one is sad at five P.M., mixing tears with bourbon, a familiar recipe.

I sight him through the crystal facets of my glass, as though in the crosshairs of a rifle, and then view our whole small world through this golden-brown collie color of booze. *Oh, Jack, be quick.* Ready, aim, fire. Boom, there goes benevolence. But he's so good, almost sacramental, so un-Western. He embodies all the gentleness, and understanding, all the empathy, that Western women think they want in their men. But they often don't, when face-to-face; many women make fun of him. I fire by tipping the glass, though my aim is insincere, unsteady; I begin to float downriver on the ice floe, in the prime whiskey of rage, not alcohol.

How can he keep talking so softly? Many of us will weep if we hear the Good Feeling song again, the hyperactive noise of that whistling toy trolley one more time. He must not see the brute contrast between his homilies and the world on the streets viewed from afar or too near; in the rehabilitation hospital beds, in the psychiatric clinics, in the overworked departments for protection of children all over the land. Perhaps I should toast him again because my daughter is happy with him, because he is as faithful as the seasons, regular as pain, usual as the indifference of doctors, and loyal as some friends. "Oh, Body," said Delmore Schwartz, "the heavy bear that goes with me." Jack lifts and drops you hard on your tush, but Fred will tuck you in. But being rescued from the claustrophobic world of inside winter, many unwalking winters, is a dazzle of relief, like the first sun after rainy, ambivalent November or seeing a star in dark sooty skies, a radiance within the weather. Even the malevolent crow cries outside the windows become exclamations, not portents, and the room expands a little, becomes interesting, if confining, more colorful, though tight in the corners, where melancholy makes its messy nest.

Looking back, I should have written letters to all the prominent figures in my flattened landscape, until an inside drift of white envelopes matched the outside white in yearned-for congruence. Perhaps people who must be reclusive should write letters to the world, as Emily Dickinson did. But do others stop because the minefield of unchosen solitude is so wide, and without boundary? Because of anomie?

However, I can be a revisionist of my own history.

*

Dear Mr. Rogers in Winter,

Share with me, reach out and touch someone, me, and pour me another Jack-Be-Daniel's, Jack-Be-Quick, and I'll toast you for your persistence and perseverance, my new 1980s Prince Summer Fall Winter Spring. I am softening toward you. Ridicule is a snake eating itself. You are cultured; you have a certain indefinable, futzy élan. Mr. Rogers, you are good for a wider world that truly needs a yeast starter for goodness. The hungry are blown around like sticks, there is Bosnia and its iron cribs of the wounded and orphaned; the spat-upon Amerasian children, the children killed in drive-by shootings. They all need you. And somewhere, someone with AIDS is watching you and your son King Friday on the Happy Train to Everything Possible Land, having slipped back on a morphine trolley, comfortable somewhere in a white warm room. Yes, Fred, the world needs you to give lessons about *honoring* and *cherishing*. But lessons with more grit, truth with teeth in it, and salted by cynicism, to help protect the children and "grown-ups," as you always call them, not adults. If you could only lean your warm monkish arms through the gray TV glass and embrace the woman stuck in the house with her daughter's crack baby, drop cash and forbearance in her thin lap; carry downstairs the elderly afraid of using piss-filled elevators. Reach out to those cutoff, impoverished, gone, and make their lives more tolerable, more textured, with your soft, too human voice. Could you have brought my grandmother out of her expanding dusty reclusion? Could you have saved my mother from her darkness with your "lite" and abundant wisdom? Could you reach to those who have slipped into even smaller rooms and shut the door, could you stop the carbon monoxide, the Seconal? Can you help me get used to not walking, to this comfortable, heated cage? Can you help those exiled by bodies or cells or neurons — by birth or yesterday's crash — trapped by grief or biochemical zigzagging? Can you make kids who have been brutalized because some-one thinks they're evil — can you make them strong at the broken places? If so, you must then package how you do it, and sell it at county fairs and in Pentecostal storefronts, in wealthy malls, in houses and in trailers.

Jack and I toast you, Mr. Rogers, who comprehend the world too sweetly. We are trying to make you into a savior, we know, but we need to keep going, and at least you're a minister.

We need you, but we need you true, urban, earthbound, and *not* singing about the beautiful day in the neighborhood.

*

Dear Skates in the Corner,
    Earthbound, snowbound.

Winter, blue ice, no sun or exercise or activity. Still watching Mr. Rogers through the eyes of Jack the Gripper. Dear Skates, Mr. Rogers has publicly announced that people can and should strive for *anything* because of intrinsic capability or beauty. But doctors and the angels of attempted repair have so far told me *not again* skating, *never again* riding, the only two "sports" I like. Besides, I only want to walk to the corner anyway. I want to skate, but won't; cutting an impression on ice is like writing with your body on a frozen page. I can't, I wail to Jack, who is deaf in both his glass ears. On the other hand, the world is full of intelligent, amazing inventions humans make for themselves, sometimes made out of the raw materials of body *and* machine. A long time ago in a supermarket, we saw a procession that seemed to have floated out of a Fellini movie, a procession that could have crossed a white beach in Sicily, so full was it of surreal grace. There was a man pushing a woman in a wheelchair, who was pushing a shopping cart attached somehow to a stroller in which a gleeful toddler sat. Now that's a magic train, more enchanted than the trolley in TV fantasyland. So, skates, can we attach your silver to my strong hands, and I'll glide across the ice on my even stronger arms? On my head?

Ice melts in the glass. That family in the market is proceeding through their history, enduring somewhere. Bravo for them. After all, I've been told only that I'll never skate, not that I can't go on imagining the glide, the warm burn against the cheeks, the body moving fast against the wind, with the wind.

*

Dear Ann Landers in the Spring,

How do you advise a grown woman so bursting against the bars of indoor routine that she writes to skates and to Mr. Rogers while her daughter watches him every season? What, Ann Landers, should she do with her passionate affinity for a minister who preaches to preschoolers and their exhausted parents, their pets dozing and farting in front of the TV?

How should he protect himself in this world, outside the TV? How can she protect her child or herself from the ice floe? When can she walk around the block, half a block?

But it's not like a blooming affair yet. One problem: she has never really liked any of his sweaters, and he's too tall and thin, and that unreal red trolley to the Land of Make-Believe would have been thrown out, renounced as too silly, to be picked up by a real garbage truck. Ann, please advise, what next?

*

Dear Elvis, in Summer Past and Present,

Mr. Rogers would have had you on his show, even with your wired druggy turbulence, along with all other musical geniuses, from the waist up only, though, just as Ed Sullivan showed you. I need your blue suede shoes; in fact, shoes are an obsession now, *walking* in glowing shoes, just as my friend in a wheelchair always dreams of wild, wanton dancing. I remember dancing to "Love Me Tender," the almost edible, combustible music that churned adolescence on, and the blue pounding shoes in the heartbreak hotel of first love: a love dead now. Much later each of us lay in different parts of the same city, but he was critically ill. We had no smooth way to reconnect as friends, to help each other. For him it was the whole ultimate heartbreak hotel, while I lived in only a small corner of one small dusty room of the place. Elvis, who knew that those teenagers, two known (unwillingly) for physical prowess and beauty before heart and intelligence, would each be trapped in their forties? He in the stopped world of terminal illness, she in the still confined world of immobility? In both cases, exiled by the bodies that used to need each other so much . . .

I drink a toast to him, to the way he slicked his hair like Elvis. *For,* as Yeats has written, *the love that fled and hid its face among the stars.*

I can sit a little now, and sitting up to the world makes me feel brand new and "snappy," as Fred would say. But how wrong John Donne was: Death *is* proud and arrogant and is the richest, meanest kid in the neighborhood who can have everything beautiful and unbeautiful, desired or not, acquiring and then acquiring again, just for the hell of it.

*

Dear Fred,

Those later summers, we used to swim and float as disability floated away; we no longer watched you every day, but

I could still hear *It's a beautiful day in the neighborhood* rippling in an underground current. Now I walk from the car to the pool. Jack is put away in honor of wine and the clearer white color of water. Often I look back and wonder why I did not write then. My fingers and hands weren't gloved in pain, were no part of the larger planet of body pain. Fred, you could see me from the TV, while the window fans rushed the musty fall air around, the sleet hit the windows, the Chair Elevator went up and down between two floors, the doorbell ringing in yet another physical therapist, with bright changing leaves behind her. The hours, the years. Why didn't I do it, when friends would say, *So much time to write?* How lucky, how *very lucky!*

It was like but not equivalent to being brain-dead in the artistic self, dear Fred, which is like a homunculus inside the larger, more placid self. There was no desire to create or embellish or even comment upon experience, as though loss of mobility had leached out the imagination at an underground level. Indifferent to mixing anything together — art stuff, paints, people, moods — I was also indifferent to transforming my quotidian world into image, or "wordliness," the words to leaping around experience like acrobats, or to growing through it like kudzu, or like simile itself. The grayness and monotony, except for Fred and daughter and husband and some friends, *un*colored everything else, and worse, took noticing and caring about noticing anyway. Sometimes, there was a yearning for writing, but, arriving at the paper, yearning went limp in prophesied futility. With all this time, people would say, you could write *two* books; but so much time was drowning me, not saving the creative anima at all.

At the rehabilitation hospital, someone told me that occasionally people with a specific kind of brain damage don't eat because they cannot will themselves to go to the full and beckoning refrigerator, even though they are hungry. The initiating and volitional part of the brain is gone, or dormant for the time being.

For me, almost phobic about comparing myself to others (having been told so many times, it could be worse; it *could*, I knew that), the words, experiences, and the concatenations of feelings, were all bulging in the refrigerator, even at the times when I was hungry to create understanding, and it was definitely time to eat. But I lay there, dumbfounded. Finally, the urge to be understood at all disappeared; and then there I was drinking the smooth Rogers and watching the delicious Jack, and not calling friends back and eating only the prime whiskey rage, saved by the repetitive duties of loving a child, helping that child. As one African proverb goes, Trouble had brought his own stool and sat in the tent, the whole tent. (You should say that on your show sometime.) Then it finally sat elsewhere — close by, not *in,* staring through the flaps, not the best neighbor in the neighborhood.

In summer, we swam and swam. And walked a little, then more, until the age of the child and the new joyous mobility meant that Fred was over, the channel changed. We were now living on two floors; I no longer worried about vandals tripping over me if they came when I had to sleep downstairs. And board by difficult board, freedom and fear were laid side by side and became a long sturdy pier that finally led to a larger vista, with a freely writing hand that grabbed the pen and used the ink.

*

Dear Horizontal Woman in Fall,
Waking in the night, not a snappy new day . . .
"I have been silent," says May Sarton, "while the great

autumn light begins, a time of change in the inner world." A time of inner, rampant change: Did May Sarton read that as she was swinging on Mr. Rogers's porch, when she was on the show one fall?

It's fall again, fall a kind of reverse pregnancy, full with foreboding.

Horizontal Woman, inside that confined world you were cocooned with a family. You were at least not *alone* in your imagined cage. Woman, you couldn't walk any distance for a long while, but you could imagine; you could swim and eat and have people take care, a husband take care, even if he was almost ruined in love by the experience. When you decided to stop ridiculing Mr. St. Rogers of Gentleheart, when you ordered the Electric Freedom Chair (and used it), and said out loud, "I am a disabled forty-two-year-old woman," you became less like a stunned panther, more like a natural creature that could go from floor to floor with ease. There were days to bless flannel, bless the old sheets on the bed in front of cheery Mr. Rogers, to bless being (provisionally) sane, to bless observing the erratic peace of nature outside, even though nature still felt inaccessible. All those years, you were in the breathing centrifuge of crisis and readjustment, along with many other people locked inside, as though in a communal snow globe, one broken-down body machine after another. *(Oh, world of white, first home of dreams.)* Then locked out from bourbon-colored leaves, then from the world of flowers and spitting new rain. Some letters to the world should have been written then just to kick over Trouble's stool, while outside nature just kept on like a vast haiku writing itself, and Mr. Rogers sang and was so full of good feeling.

PART THREE

TOWARD

THE WORLD

Chaplinesque

No matter how desperate the predicament is,
I am always very much in earnest about checking my cane,
straightening my hat, and fixing my tie,
even though I have just landed on my head.

— *Charlie Chaplin*

CANDY NOISE / TOYLAND

Water pistols, dolls that dribble food, balls that bounce themselves forever on rubber stubs, hyperactive toys that screech,
pee, fight, duel, sleep, whimper, and sing at this vast toy store,
where overly sweet music, like candy noise, comes out of pores
in the ceiling and into ours, where it causes instant irritation
and belligerence. *Play that song one more time and we'll spit our
bubble gum at the speakers, wherever they are.*

I have never been happier: for seven years I've wanted to
come here, but couldn't. Even my own combativeness makes

me happy, even all the visual cacophony of toys/color/money, exorbitantly dressed adults, a thousand-dollar full-size stuffed retriever, five hundred kinds of teddy bears. Even the floor, expansive floor . . .

Where's a chair? I had asked. *In the back of the store*, she said. But I don't want to be in the back of the store, so I'll lie down right here, on this lovely green rug, with the dolls and games and sunglasses with bulging, rotating eyes attached.

I'll get you a stepladder. Maybe that will do. She was holding ten hand puppets. I was still happy.

The carpet was cushiony and smelled like lavender room fragrance. Charlie and I smelled it together: he held a daisy, I watched the infectious attractive greed of children and the worn ostentatious greed of the adults.

When she came back with a stepladder, it was a hard call: the floor provided a panoramic view of shoes, those self-bouncing balls, toddlers purring excited faces in my direction. I stayed there.

Later, when I called the store's customer service office, far less happy, they mentioned the chairs — in the back, which I knew. (Perfect for exile, isolation, feelings of difference, away from the noise, the glitter, the fun.) And two on either side of the escalator: isolation, but less. You certainly couldn't shop with your child *there* at the top of the stairs. What did they expect? That those "disabled" want only to sit, not play, not enjoy? Finally, when I asked why there couldn't be chairs throughout the store for those who just have trouble standing, she said, quotably, "It's just not part of the decor." Store/decor: was I included in the decor?

Store/decor: I had never thought of *that*, when I walked out that happy night, twirling my cane like a baton, and along came Charlie down the street, twirling his cane like a windmill, flapping his large platypusian shoes. He winked, I winked. Candy noise, he said. Hello, I said, and we went off down the fancy glowing street, through the City Lights, I half walking, half lurching, and he duck-footing in the gorgeous snow.

TRAPPED BY ZUCCHINI

I regard town after town after town one afternoon on the Amtrak ride to Cleveland, the sleeping car shimmying, flatly musical, as it clacks over the long northern forehead of upstate New York and Ohio. In the narrow bottom bunk where I lie, I wonder what to do. Set beside me, just beside my nose, is the primordial slime of tomatoes, yellow squash, and zucchini, sadistically called ratatouille, with the nursing home odor of vegetable steam wafting at me: Amtrak room service. The jittery train is too unstable for me to stand up and balance between the "bed" and washbasin. There's no place to move the stuff, which would ooze over the edge of the plastic plate, and there's no room to sit up. I am there, as they say, for the duration, trapped by the so-called food. There is no escape. But the hungry Tramp would eat the stuff, lick his chops, finger his mustache, and tilt off drunkenly, as though what he had just eaten had turned to happy gin in his happy gut.

AFTER-DINNER PLUNGE

Try it, everyone has said. They are fabulous for backs, these waterbeds: just sink in like a ship, let it mother you, rock you into an infinity of painlessness. You can chuckle and snuggle and dream of Caribbean warmth: of dolphin comfort, skin to smooth bedspread, over the ripples of water-satiety, satori.

Then I am sinking, sinking, my spine is welded to the warm plasticity, the ripples are like waves. I have beginning wavelets and tremors of motion sickness. But this is no ocean liner; one can go ashore. I am a person flailing and laughing and floating.

But I can't get up over the hard edge of the bed frame. When I try, the mattress sinks back. The mattress is so full, so depthful, there's no purchase: I lean and fall back into the pillowy ocean of the bed. Will it have to be drained? Can we call the fire department to hoist the laughing woman up from this squishiness and then back down to the hard, adored earth? Where is Charlie? He needs to figure out a rambunctious choreography to get me out, help me rise. He holds out his arm draped with a waiter's cloth: Madam, can I help? (I needed the waiter on the train.) Now I need a life buoy.

I do rise like Venus, I fly like Daedalus, to the arms helping me out, to stand on the floor, one timid foot after another. This is the floor, the ground: *I am the floor, thy floor. Thou shalt have no other solids before me.*

I would kiss the ground, but it seems too far away. I laugh at my predicament, at what would have been the headline: Woman Spends the Duration of Her Life in Waterbed. Survives with Chaplin's Help.

GINGERBREAD

It is December 23, 1989: the *Joy of Cooking* in front of me, the Joy of Snowing outside. Gingerbread people to be made: a matter of proving it can be done on the floor. The girl (mine) and her cousin (boy) do not yet read, but pretend to follow the recipe. All the necessary ingredients in the chaotic kitchen have been assembled hours before because there is only a little time to stand up: first to get vanilla, flour, the ginger, then back to the floor, then up at the table to sit and mix with them. *When we gonna cut them? Where we gonna roll them?* the skeptical cousin probably asks.

On the floor, of course, the adapted girl answers, probably. *Of course,* as though everyone does things this way, don't they?

So on the floor we go, a heap of found domestic sculpture: cookie cutters, rolling pin, a dust of dry flour everywhere, a paste of wet flour on faces, beautiful heads bent over the resistant dough, which is difficult for me to roll out on the floor, but a breeze for them. Flour on my head, dough in my mouth, I sing, *This is what I'm supposed to do.* I won't be stopped.

There's sugar on the floor which didn't quite mix in, more flour that dulls the white-gold shine on both of their identically shaped heads: we did it, we did it. They give up rolling and cutting figurative shapes and try expressionism: pounding, attaching limbs, eyes, pressing wildness into the lumpiness, until all the so-called figures look completely odd and joyous. Exhausted from rolling on the floor, in the flour, I put them in the oven, and the fragrance booms out like some ecstatic explosion of smell. I am the Ur-Bear, the mother bear, and this is my cave, my messy dominion. Things come out of the oven like sweet, sweet cowpies with legs and chocolate chip warts.

They don't taste good: they taste like dry fortune cookies with ginger in them because I forgot half the sugar and one egg in my hurry to get the sitting part over with. But we eat some of them: after all, they are artifacts from a new and daring Floor Expedition. How the cousins smile: smiling is their trade.

I am in love with the cowpies, the gingered house, the flour in various small nests in my hair, all Christmases before (upright) and not (horizontal) rolled into this one lush Happening of an afternoon, with laughter and failure and farce. Tomorrow, out go the cowpies that the children don't want — to the hungry winter birds.

Charlie tosses a few in the air, juggles them, throws some sugar at them, eats twelve because he's a hungry Tramp, twitches his nose, gobbles more, convincing us these are the best ginger gender-free cookie people, the best and the silliest — all this in a large memorious snow globe to be shaken ten years from now, and admired.

AFTER LUNCH

Quite a few years later, I escape for a drive.

Then I have to escape from the car: I am locked *inside* because of a series of miniglitches that finally propel me to the mechanic's, where I sit imprisoned in the auto, a fly on flypaper. The stubborn door won't open from the inside: the electric window won't open enough for my arm to reach out with a key to unlock the same door from the outside.

The obvious solution? Get out of the car on the other side, walk around, open the door. Perfectly logical. But I can't bend my body to rise over the gear shaft. I humbly beseech the mechanic to let me out and fix the lock of the frigging car, and quick, because I have to go to the bathroom and what am I supposed to do if the car catches fire, for instance?

And how far is the bathroom? While the mechanic takes his time answering, I wonder: What if we had an accident and got locked inside?

For Christ's sake, too far. I stand there, wondering, wishing my cane had a razor on the end, or a hammer, like James Bond would have. Of course, it's not the mechanic's fault that it's so far to walk to the next building. I debate.

Now in true distress, downcast, I see Charlie Chaplin mushing his mouth against the car window, as though he's in the large, bright aquarium of the real world, and I'm outside it, trapped in the car. He flattens his nose, kisses the window, flutters his long giraffe-like lashes, putting himself square between me and the bewildered mechanic, and a gentle laughter falleth like manna from heaven: mine. And mine the laughter that helps me wait until the door is open; woman escapes, Charlie moves off in the direction of a warm saloon, fish-kissing the air as he walks, and she never forgets him.

Fourteen Ways of Looking
at the Horizontal Woman

(after Wallace Stevens)

ONE

What does he think about all day long, this working man who
ferries wheelchairs from one end of this immense airport to the
other? Does he wear the correct shoes for cushioning such hard
physical labor, or does OSHA provide him with advice on er-
gonomic pushing? Does he get bored with his job as quickly as
others do? He must like some people, loathe others. Or is it just
one long indistinguishable march down the polished steel corridors, with the wheelchairs becoming part of the arms' history,
as unremarkable as opening a quart of orange juice, or closing
the garage door at night?

When he gets the horizontal woman to the gate, she says,
"I'm out of here," starting to rise, capable of walking the rest

of the way now. "Not here, sweetie, we're not quite there," he says. Bristling, she asserts, "No really, I *want to walk*, I just need it for the distances." (This part-hitching-a-ride, part-walking makes others suspicious.) "Let me out," she repeats. Haughtily, he says. "Oh, *I* know. You're one of them that hates the Disability." Well, yes, but who the hell *loves* disability or injury of any sort? She starts to fight, but he has turned, and his tired back moves away to take another one who hates the Disability. Without pushing the squeaky machines, he seems taller and, in his gray uniform, whistles "Some Enchanted Evening." Should there be a Love Your Disability Club, membership none?

TWO

"Others just manage," the Voice says, referring to that last privacy, the bladder, over the phone. Why don't they have a bathroom on the first floor of the old theater, the horizontal woman had dared to wonder, and it is explained that she can take a freight elevator down to the bathroom in the basement, a real privilege. What does Voice say next? "Others do it."

"Others do it," Voice repeats, accusingly. How? By not drinking for six hours before, the horizontal woman calculates, thirsty already.

Voice says, "They figure out a way." And then backed up behind the abrupt and insensitive Voice, the horizontal woman sees an endless line of people in wheelchairs, people who cannot use stairs for whatever reason (MS, cerebral palsy, age), parched and hot, either uncomfortably "holding" it or descending into the shabby, brown dark of the freight elevator to the basement.

THREE

What does her child think (what does any child feel, even when the erratic rhythms of adjustment are years old?), watching a parent of previously robust energy and joie de everything being physically helped to do something as usual as getting up the stairs? *Our Town* is in the gym: four flights of stairs, no elevator, two men lifting the parent under the arms, and all the other children watching, and the parent (*that* mother, her *mother*) feeling like vulnerable meat between two hooks. But no, the men are respectful, full of dark humor, gentle. She gets there, she participates in whatever she can no matter the cost, no matter what the interior trembling at the embarrassment of being carried in all her new sedentary fat, at an elementary school that has no elevator. Our town, child's school, her body.

FOUR

"Well, what's *that* thing for?" asks the manager.

"That *thing* is a cane chair for people who have trouble standing up," says the horizontal woman.

She's at a store in a tired strip mall with all its old purple neon signage glowing and broken off. Here's the Dress Warehouse, a concrete wilderness of slacks, sweaters, shirts. Who would want dresses that carry the scent of concrete and storage and too-manyness? Well, she does need *many* items, so she has unfolded the contraption for a long look. Shopping is so difficult that it's best to find a huge place with many choices and plant herself there, or an intimate place where people will bring merchandise to her. The seat is dangerous, though useful beyond measure: it means freedom to select, to be able to be a consumer again, after so many years.

There are three skimpy aluminum legs and a seat just large enough for an elf, where she had been sitting in order to easily twirl a rack of skirts. When she became aware of eyes arrowing her, she asked, "What are you staring at?" The frail-looking manager finally said, "Well, people sometimes crouch down low like that and stuff *stuff* in their bags."

"Do you see me crouching?" This woman thinks she is shoplifting. The comment makes her feel, frankly, murderous.

So then why does the horizontal woman blush? "I'm writing the company. What's your name?" But she's already on her way out of the store, presto, burning with outrage, skin prickling as the August heat melts the asphalt.

"Save up for the important battles," her husband says. "They all are," she says, and they are all inside, and the battles do battle with each other until it feels like an unedited chapter in Tolstoy. May the Dress Warehouse burn, she hopes, may all real shoplifters prevail. May the manager toss and turn tonight when she thinks of that Criminal Accessory, the cane chair. May she dream a flock of cane chairs attack her like Hitchcock's birds, may she never wake from dreams of all the shoplifters overtaking the entire store, crouch by crouch, stuffing *stuff* until all the hideous stock is gone.

FIVE

Only the room, so near the operating room, was requested. The rest is benevolence, kindness pure but crisply delivered, not condescending. Business-like, the nurses bring the horizontal woman what she doesn't even ask for: ice packs, coffee, a portable phone for calling relatives. With clarity, her need to be with her child at the hospital has been seen: a very great need. Her mother has come to help her be there, wheeling the chair. I can't be there, she told the hospital, unless there's a place to lie down: otherwise she would be far away from her child in surgery, the distance magnifying worry, the worry in turn making distance greater. The nurses saw how devastating this would be.

Now their nylon uniforms rustle above her; they look at her uncritically, even without curiosity. After all, this lying down is only one posture of motherhood, and they've seen hundreds: abject, joyful, bruising, praying, forced on the shoals of despair, climbing the apex of hope, blind with love or fury. Through the metal forest of metal chair legs — around the conference table in this room that belongs solely, this day, to her — she watches their blessed white shoes and tights. Thank you.

Tomorrow as her daughter recovers from a tonsillectomy — minor surgery, but to parents, the absence of their child during anesthesia is a gape of terror — the horizontal woman will be permitted to lie on the bed all day with her four-year-old, though people are changing IVs, taking temperatures, delivering Jell-O, and she is an obstacle to their efficiency.

The soft surprise of this enormous kindness gives an aftershape, a roundness, to the days following, days to hold warmly in remembering hands, like cashmere wool or bread.

Home with much help, the horizontal woman is in charge of convalescence: like her, the child is mostly lying down for a while. Side by side, they lie, mother and healing child, mother tending and grateful for those hands that gave, and the clear nurses' eyes that saw plain raw need and did not judge.

SIX

Before she dresses for an interview, she assesses how much the skirt will ride up on her lying-down legs. Once there, she will look at the admissions person, smile, offer some minimal explanation, then proceed to lie down on the carpet or couch, talking from there about her daughter's need for a progressive creative education. According to individual character, according to willingness to accept the explanation for her lying down, the directors are either overly warm, or detached, scrutinizing her for other "problems," psychological perhaps. (Do any think this is some clever ruse to jump the competition?) She will always wonder if horizontalism affected decisions, in either direction. *How unfortunate for the family, strange woman, brave woman, why can't she get some help?* What *did* they think? Odd story was probably the usual conclusion: certainly won't fill any quota, any usual disability category, and what about the elevator situation?

SEVEN

Here's a tree so filled with thick white blossoms that it looks as if clumps of snow or egrets have nested in it. She is peaceful here, lying on the wool blanket always folded in her bag. Often she wishes for a blanket made of cool water, or serenity.

The birds are hungry: don't they know there's pumpkin seed on this plate, free for the taking? Can she walk the distance to the car if it gets any hotter? The others are inside at the reception, and occasionally look out at her: she's a kind of summer still life here, but then three men walk toward her — not complete strangers, not well known either. Now they are almost standing on the blanket; it feels threatening, not the way it would be if she could run. "Well," says one of them, "isn't this just the sexiest thing?" Or was it, "What a voluptuous pose"?

To answer is to comply, to allow them to continue in some way. Not to answer — or to provide rebuke — is difficult also, and so she's stuck and momentarily speechless with fury. *Birds, come help, let's have magical intervention, as in South American stories. Fly me away. Drop your lovely shit on them.*

"Just lying under the trees, having a grand time?" he says. *That* phrase heats the air. When she speaks, a sizzle of steam accompanies her words. "Just go back inside and party away. I've got a back injury." She hates to provide explanation then: her body has to go public. Her words are thin and stiff, in contrast to the trees in the wind, blowsy and silky-looking, high summer trees; shivering leaves; and humiliations like this are as numerous as the shadowy interstices between the leaves, and best forgotten, but how should one?

EIGHT

At a children's holiday fair, a well-dressed father circles her for a long time, viewing her body from every angle, like someone seriously scrutinizing an exotic animal in a cage. Then he goes off to a greater distance in a corner of the gym and does *exactly* the same thing, closing in, asking sarcastically, bitterly, "Tired, are you? Are we *disturbing* you?" Later, while notes of "Jingle Bells" and the dreidel song fill her ears with the easy warmth and goodness of enthusiastic children, she admires the shellac on the floor, feels grounded by imperfectly lilting voices that distract her from the impending army of her tears, and the gray winter months ahead.

And what, she wonders, sharpens his bitterness? Perhaps it is detachment, or a sorrowful acquaintance with a more major illness or more massive injury that makes him criticize her. Perhaps it's plain stupidity.

NINE

The airport carpet is steam-cleaned every day, but it is still well steeped in shoe grease, baby shit from diaper changing, bubble gum, coffee and beer, perfume that falls out of traveling cases — and other spilled evidence of human preoccupation. Consequently, when she lies down, the horizontal woman lays a green wool scarf for protection, beside the wheelchair and cane: a deliberate arrangement for telling the narrative to passersby who might wonder why a healthy-looking woman and a small child are on the floor in a public space.

Suddenly she hears two voices: *Look at her. Isn't that just something. Aren't you just the height of luxury there?* She looks around for height, for luxury, and finally for a weapon, but her eyes land on her daughter's bewildered face, where they need to stay, more than on these strangers' misguided prattle. She thinks, *Yes, I'm so luxurious down here I could fart Chanel.* But, instead, she tells her daughter not to worry, the women are just silly, aren't they?

And what would the women have done if she had looked poor and tattered, or had been Latina or black? Would they have called Security, instead of just mounting this small, nervous assault?

TEN

Whenever they travel, she is like some strange Cleopatra on her makeshift bed in the back. When the car stops at a red light, she's often suddenly eye-level with the surprised drivers beside her. Caught like a fugitive in a sudden encounter, the horizontal woman turns her gaze away from them: the grinning adolescents, women with curious pointing children, older people who catch a bit of their future more frail selves in the supine woman beside them, wondering as they avert their fearful, kindly eyes.

ELEVEN

Fourth of July party, lots of social workers, therapists, children, dogs. There are no fireworks here, thank God, for she has always hated the violent noise, the shock of display, the scattering apart of hot particles (like a marriage going askew) only to reassemble in design: the potential for misfiring, injury, recreational catastrophe. A gentle and genteel gathering on the hot brown grass, people with a few too many gin and tonics.

She's placed herself where she can get a panoramic view of conversations — the configurations of people nodding and whispering and leaning too close or away from each other.

On this floor, she's content to watch the festive children beyond the picture window. A contemplative child swings alone in the yard; she watches him, fascinated. Like that child, this horizontalism has left her more singular, no longer a gregarious socializer extraordinaire. But as a spectator she's happy now, in a summer daze about other summers: the milky smell of mowed grass, the way her uncle woke them up every morning with

Chopin. From far away, the words slur above her, slowly breaking through her thick reverie. *Oh help me help me help me, I've fallen and I can't get up.* In a falsetto voice, the man above her is imitating the Lifeline ad on TV, in which an elderly woman is stuck alone and terrified on the floor, will probably be stuck there forever to suffer because her guilty family hasn't bought Lifeline. (As the actress must also suffer the humiliation of doing this degrading commercial over and over.)

Now he's laughing, mercilessly and idiotically at once. What would work better, mace or a water pistol filled with bear piss? Is he a social worker or is he a sociopath? Perhaps he hates his old unfortunate mother, or age in general? To insult or not: whatever takes less energy, finding the right zing or living with the guilt of passivity, letting it go. He staggers away, Mr. Ha Ha, Mr. Spoiler. Help, she thinks. No more parties, no more gatherings. Just enclosure and privacy, like that child's on the swing. Just being around those who know too well this kind of careless remark, and can toss one back like a lit firecracker.

TWELVE

The crescent-shaped balcony for handicapped seating measures about twelve by six, and it is luxurious, a fine reversal for a change. Below are the hundreds of newly refurbished seats, with Wedgwood blue frosting and gold curlicues decorating the woodwork. As opposed to a megaplex, this is a cozy, small-town movie house, a manageable movie house. The curls and the bald heads shine up. She sees the solitary and those embracing: kisses furtive and not, people filing in timidly or obstreperously, not yet suspecting the voyeur in the balcony who notes their smallest habits. Past the gawky adolescent ticket takers, the white recliner has arrived and sits in its welcoming sling-curve, ready to accommodate her joy of being out.

With popcorn, she reclines and waits for furtive, predictable looks upward. When they first spot her — but not the wooden cane beside her — she guesses by the slight contempt on their faces that they might think: *What does that woman think she is doing, taking a seat from the handicapped.* (Some even giggle and point.) When she looks back, the spectators sometimes look instantly away. She tries to make her gazes fierce and proud, often fails, is disappointed at another evening possibly ruined. Why can't she learn not to care? Teach us to care and not to care, said Eliot, teach us to sit still. She's a slow learner in this: she hates being so conspicuous.

The movie starts. She loves the glitter and jazz of the lit-up screen more now than as a child; for four years she could not go, before she found the chair. Her simple chair is beloved, has endowed her with magical freedom, even transcendence, here above the crowd. The critics below are like wardens in their vigilance. But for now, just now, the old red velvet curtains framing the stage, and the movie about to unfold, are more potent than their anger. And she hopes that some from the hospital will be pleasured so, like this, in doing one previously impossible thing.

THIRTEEN

The steaming piles of food are exactly wrong for such heat. But tonight is the chosen, worked-for time. The horizontal woman is going to sit through a whole meal, instead of finishing on one of the couches in an adjoining room. Urgently, a waitress comes so close that her sweat is pungent, so close she's within hitting distance. Next, the waitress grabs the cane away from her without warning, and says, "Hey, you don't need that here on vacation," looking livid and inscrutable. The adults at the table advise yelling for the owners. "What do you mean?" is all the horizontal woman can summon; she is on display, insulted by a college kid unaware of her own fury (and it *is* fury on that red face, so close). Year after year they've both been here at this resort. Year after year, has this young invader been building a case against her odd "disablement"? Has the girl dreamed of "fixing" her with this sudden shocking gesture?

The piles of turkey and potatoes and green beans blur into a beige wash. The lake goes gray and rainy; the boats are a wet smudge. When the horizontal woman tells the story later, the gusto for ridiculing the young woman fades. What floats up, as if from some murky part of the summer water, is disdain for her own inability to speak up, her own hammering sadness about the public eye.

FOURTEEN

I watch the horizontal woman, now on the tarp, while her daughter skates and skates into her own ineluctable freedom of body: twisting, falling, falling, sweeping, lighting us, free. She is warm, although she's reclining on the cold bench. She's laughing because she's *there*, not home, not at the hospital. Next to her is a man in a wheelchair, there every week too. As usual, she feels a kind of subtle guilt; he's in the chair all the time, she now uses it only for the big distances. Though she doesn't know his medical condition, she feels companionable with this stranger. Is he warm enough, she wonders, then remembers that he takes care of himself. To ask would be an intrusion on his privacy. He is watching his two children skate far away from him, as distant as health, then in close to touch his hand, his powerful father hand, as momentarily her own child will spin in, hot and red-cheeked, to say, *Watch me, watch me,* in the false cold of late September at an indoor skating rink.

Do I Go Out, You Ask

> Shame is the recognition of the fact that I am the
> object the Other is looking at and judging.
>
> — *Jean-Paul Sartre*

M. parked the car and I waited in the wheelchair, which I took
for self-defense and for the short trip from the curb to the bar. I
had called the restaurant earlier, so the spectacle of a woman
lying down wouldn't agitate the maître d' too much, and had
prepared a "presentation" of myself to be more acceptable, less
conspicuous, to the public: a longer dress that wouldn't sneak
up. When I got to the bar, the brocade couch looked beautiful
under the beveled windows, the gray-pink glass with green
petals marked unevenly by the divisions of lead. Holiday lights
made random constellations on the Norfolk pines: I felt rever-
ent and unencumbered. I ordered a drink. Out like this for the
first time in five years was as exciting as heading toward Rome,

Florence, Cairo. But this place, the rich brown darkness of a place called Not Home, felt dangerous, with a freedom so excessive it was like the taste of lemon or chocolate — explosive and big. It was true: I still had an enjoying self, and that self was becoming too ecstatic.

But then someone started to stare. Being stared at somehow creates a sense of shame, as though the soul suddenly assumes a face and must hide it, turning away wordless, cast off. And how could I allow another stranger, this time a well-dressed, all-gray businessman, to cause such commotion for me? Even with the wheelchair there, for context, the eyes of people still searched me out. What is that woman doing lying in *our* bar? This time I stared back, forcing boldness out of *its* hiding place. It was an animal confrontation: I was also asking for mercy. *Please, I am asking you, do not violate me. I know I look odd, but get on with it, accept it.* I wanted to punish him, for his face to go slack with embarrassment. He just walked away.

Sentimentalists have told me this horizontalism arouses fear of frail old age or illness. What it also provokes is rudeness, contempt for the imperfect, and the urge to treat the "different person" like a large puppy or a voiceless alien. But what is it that affronts them? Of course, we all know it upsets propriety. How many times do you see a woman lying down on the window seat in an expensive bar? But anyone could also see that the world was going on politely anyway: no tables turned over, no bottles broken, no needles, no shopping bags or overflowing carts. The spectacle of it was quiet, just a woman in a hotel with a man, sometime in late November. (And what if it *does* violate spatial expectations to see an adult horizontal? Other eyes could see an odalisque, Matisse would love the scene, Manet would have me at a luscious indoor picnic, Seurat would pointillize the light here and the shape of the mirrored bar.)

And then it happens, the moment that always comes like a canyon to cross. I have to go to the bathroom. M. has to push the flimsy collapsible wheelchair across the whole vast lobby and, as we speed past onlookers, I look up at the ceiling to avoid their eyes. (Shame again. Why? What color is shame? What is the shame about being in a wheelchair? It is still just so new, being pushed, transported like cargo.) Cherubs are up there, and angels and more cherubs who curl their fists around bunches of fat pink roses, up across that dome of unnatural blue. What would it be like up there, rococo and full, and not here below, tethered to earthbound-ness? I wish for gold to snow down on me, for wheelchairs that fly. I could bear many more years of not walking if there was just this promise of spaciousness, and exotic pleasure if I could do this every month, let's say.

Speeding through the lobby, I suddenly felt as if I were flying on the ceiling, but poised for danger, like a person about to go off a gold windowsill. I was in deep new love with space, with vaulted ceilings, and was precipitously happy, fearfully happy. It would all soon be taken away. I'd be back home, where it is seasonless, with no gold or cherubs, just waiting, being driven back and forth to the hospital, without even the excitement of a trip to the bathroom at a hotel.

At dinner I told the waiter about my joy at being out after so many years. He was of course unmoved. He was from Florence, my dreamed destination, the city of Madonnas and sienna light and mattress factories. "We went there on our honeymoon," I told him. (We walked and ran and made smooth love.) "Nice," he said. "Do you want to order?" I was back there, with the dolorous church bells, the mink heads hanging from second-story fur workshops, causing the stink in the beautiful streets. But then I see the way it would be now, a middle-aged woman stuck in a *pensione* in the city, unable to navigate the difficult cobblestones, cut off from drifting through the rich shocking contrasts of that city, and then cutting further through this image, the husband walking the streets alone, coming back to his jealous ghost-wife at the end of his full day. (I have no mercy for myself, this *is* what I see.) But even her desolation and envy cannot dull this evening.

As we ate there that night (now I can sit up for fifteen minutes as opposed to last year's ten, and you *can* eat a fancy meal in fifteen minutes), the pianist started bubbling Gershwin and the room grew voluptuous and overwhelming. The pianist was no genius, but it was new music glittering in a new room, and I was levitated; my mind stood up like an evangelist at a prayer meeting. *Amen yes I am saved I have arrived at a temple and Yes Lord the quality of mercy is not strained, now it falleth through music like manna, the music, the food, the rapture, the birds of paradise on the table, the cherubs, the great gobs of gold on the ceiling.* Then the heavy sweetness of too many emotions squeezed like a winepress until the tears flew out, scattered everywhere. I had binged and was paying for it. I was weeping in public; people were staring.

See how she cries in this dignified restaurant, how she hides her face behind the too intricate flower arrangement. Where the tears fall on the tablecloth, the damask turns a darker pink, a deep dusty pink. More sloppy tears fall into the artichoke soup, the sole with grapes, the chocolate gâteau. Like a mole who scurries out too fast from the tunnel to light, I was hurt by a too muchness. The joy was beating me up, destroying my difficult balance.

And as I went back home that night, I was blinded not by that brightness, but by the glaring prospect of the monotony ahead. By confinement, by fear of falling on ice, of not walking, of falling if I tried, of being snowbound in my own mind: January, February, March. Sometimes I would make up reasons to call people, just to talk. The hours and months of falling snow seemed deadly, ice the enemy, mobility far off. I am not saved. The music no longer was falling like manna. The quality of mercy is indeed still strained, and seems to be falling away.

Since you asked . . .

Instructions to the Painter

Capture the way the light slips through the old copper screens on the porch where the horizontal woman is watching the other two drift out in the canoe, farther and farther away, past the scruffy middle island, the first destination of this July adventure. Paint that canoe, the cheap old aluminum one, with enduring oils, with strokes of an impasto, and then do the granite-colored waves that slap it, tip it, right it again. Then take on the challenge of the inscrutable mottled sky, striped with pink cirrus and fierce upcoming weather. (They are tranquil out there, stopped for a moment, looking for a stray loon, or for the humpy rocks that abruptly surface like the backs of leathery hippopotami.)

Oh summertime, summertime, E. B. White said, *patterns of life indelible, the fade-proof lake, the woods unshatterable.* Farther out beyond these two women, paint the odd islands, mostly privately owned; in fact, only the truly rich live here, or renters like those of us who come each year. What keeps it peaceful and pure is also what keeps it exclusive, keeps the others with their loud boats away from the water, so it's a moral paradox. Though we rent, we are part of the excluding, we who are all egalitarian and believe nature should be for everyone, except those motorboaters and hunters and snowmobilers.

The watched women hunch together in the milky mist that is like an emanation from the lake, like odorless incense. Their frequent journeys from the dock get longer and more complex, and farther away from the horizontal woman — healthy, exciting pursuits, their travels to the lake's reclusive corners, their miles of robust swimming from dock to dock in the sometimes choppy water — the usual "sports" for sturdy bodies. These are seductive, glinting waters for imaginative limbs to challenge and explore. The women have the innocence of those whose bodies have never been prevented for long from doing what they want, and the commonly shared privilege of *not* worrying about inability to walk or sit (or to gather the courage not to complain constantly). Their bodies are not yet seen as burdens or longtime cheats. The two are enviable for that; the bitter but reasonable woman on the porch knows that their friendship is partly fueled by shared vigor. They will pull away from her, won't they, because she is horizontal, often in one place, dull to the eye and ear? Isn't that part of an unconscious tribal habit of leaving the weak behind? However, to think of herself as weak is an oxymoron; only in legs and back, not in the always vigorous, always protesting spirit.

The woods, *unshatterable* beside the porch, are crowded with some trees just born, light green and healthy and some waning or dying; raspberry bushes blooming, red oak, black oak; all living streaks of color. Then conifers and bare maples struck by lightning, which look like biblical elders on a sere plain, ready to be etched in deep black for posterity. The quaking aspens, the basswood, the mountain ash — or is it the white ash that makes a skittery noise with its leaves flattening out like legs against the porch screen, complicating and rendering the view differently each time? Here and there the view is obstructed with these strange "spider-flowers," as the woman calls them, splayed to make an eerie, though beautiful design. Past these flowers, the other women seem to fade into a hazy green infinity, the miles of lake that stretch unperturbed.

Now paint in closer detail their strong arms that paddle the frosted dark water. Is there an exact shade for the color of everyone's good intentions, kind hearts? A sharper color for the sound of voices discovering something like deepening friendship? The sound of these voices travels with too much clarity back over the water, to her. Are they discussing her? *What about the depression? Will she get better? We have a right to our friendship too.* This friendship, she knows, has taken root and sustenance after all the togetherness of renting this house, of going off hiking, exploring, shopping the strange impoverished yard sales of this part of New Hampshire; she's been on the porch or in the bedroom mostly. She knew both of them first, separately, seemingly forever; she was the conduit for their friendship to begin, but she never knew it would flourish beyond her. Can anyone paint how slowly the seeds of trust and loyalty change? Turned one way in the sun, they seem barely touched. One more turn, and yes, there are marks of shrivel, a wornness and thinness on one side or the other. The change can't be unthought, unexperienced, can it? (She says to herself: *this is hardly deep exile here; this porch fronts mountains that are a green nexus of thousands of creatures and plants, all to look at.*)

These two were like "found sisters," like "found" art or poetry — green glass shaped like an anvil on the beach, a setting of headlines that accidentally flash an esoteric wisdom. In the *pattern of life indelible,* where is the prefiguration for smaller losses, this voyage away from her, as they push off from the shore; or for this receding of her confidence and joy? A quiet loss is part of the pattern, the thread that pulls out, but does not yet ruin the design. Just as pattern and ecology are companion principles, intrinsic to each other, and just as ecology of the lake, the land, the trees, the soil, the world, is threatened by sudden unpredicted change, so too is the ecology of friendship. When something is added or taken away, some strange warmth or acid cold, something enters the subsoil; when something shifts in the strata, the new element balances or endangers the whole system, irrevocably or momentarily. Apply a darkish oil for irrevocable, for that word is threatening and thick, but use a soft watercolor for what might pass, or change.

Irrevocable or momentary: damage or soften?

"I am watercolor, I wash off," says Anne Sexton in a poem on a different subject, and the porch-woman feels like watercolor, not suitable for framing. She wants to wash off the burdensome ahedonistic body soon. *Watercolor:* other people seem to be in the vivid oil of vivid physical health, doing activities that look to her incandescent. In the few photos of those years, she has been either absent, or blurred, hiding behind others. People have not, in general, taken her picture.

Paint the dusty light again, coming in serrated patterns through the spider-flowers; afternoon now, and the lake, beloved lake, has changed from an early haze of bronze to a dark, almost threatening blue. On the porch, light falls over apple cores, books, maps, *Vogue* and *Poetry* magazines, the special Princess Di issue of *People*, the bird book, binoculars, old Kleenex, Scrabble, Monopoly, the cane, the white chair, Molson bottles, creamed coffee that is undergoing moldy transformations, melting chocolate, an old paint set that is part of the whole messy compost of a mostly happily shared house. Glaze this part over and over with sepia, so that these artifacts of joy, leisure, and interests both refined and vulgar — these plain icons of daily life and daily obsessions — deepen in color and do last through the many kind and unkind years.

Now, closer in, her hair should be painted reddish, with tough skeins of white, half blond and graying pewter, the tangled and wiry haze of middle-aged blond hair: hair to be proud of, to toss in the face of age or disability. Like a cartoonist then, draw in incremental frames the big, awkward motion of how she gets in the car to drive down to the water, in order to sit in a canoe, so she can watch the two more intimately, become connected through water to them — as though they were all in the same amniotic pool.

There, the gentle animal that is the water noses against the canoe, rocks it like a big cradle. She trails her hand in the silky *easiness* of the green tea-colored ripples, hearing the strange call of the eloquent but stupid loon that is worshipped on this lake. She paddles the boat in place.

As dusk comes on, take the large brush and paint in gouache, the *unfading* lake, now less turbulent; paint the *unshatterable woods* teeming with all its populations.

Paint the woman in the canoe trying to reverse the ecology of small but seismic losses, trying to shake away the chill of beginning estrangements. Her eyes will darken to navy blue, and her otherworldly hair always rendered in oil, not water-color. At least this hair can be seen from very far away, brighter than a yellow-and-white-beaded headdress, or a tropical bird never before seen in New Hampshire — hair that would fly behind her like a flaring banner, if she could run.

Shoes

Every morning
the world
is created.

— from "Morning Poem," Mary Oliver

And where could you go after the first few years?

My daughter wants to buy new shoes. I tell her *if* there's a parking space close in, *if* the aisles of the store are not too long, *if* I feel up to it. *If,* that short word with the long tight control over her life with me. I don't want you to be disappointed if it turns out we can't do it today, I tell her. She accepts this conditionality from me — or seems to, but what does this constant tentativeness do to her? For her, everything is contingent on pain, or the absence of it, pain the figure that shadows us everywhere.

But, with a voluptuous sense of free will and utility, I later drive my child to get shoes; both of us know this is so rare that the joy is sharpened. In the car, there is a kind of hopeful suspense. Will I be able to get to the door? Will I walk too much this time and not even know it until later, when my body betrays me? But all this is tempered by the sweet possibility that I can actually do something for her, fulfill a wish, grant her a partly upright mother for a while this afternoon, instead of contorting myself for the illusion of normalcy as I do on playgrounds, where I lie on the dirt while she swings and does the slide. Or when I go to her school and lie on the floor for skits. She will now have, at the shoe store, a mother who acts "usual." We have a finding-a-parking-space song, "Cross your fingers, cross your toes." This morning we nervously sing it.

Finding one feels like soothing luck. We locate a salesgirl (will she think I'm loony or lazy?), and I hope she will be decent — not condescending, not disbelieving, not hostile — when I give my usual explanation: "I have to lie on the bench. Can you help her? I can't walk over to the size thirteens. Maybe you can help find her something plain, then take the bill to the desk because I can't wait in line." Is this too much to ask? The anger and fear behind this monotonous recital makes me want to weep. I'm like a child waiting for the principal as I wait for the salesgirl's reaction. (If only my skeptical friends who try to catch me up in the retelling of these stories — as though it *couldn't possibly* be as difficult to do simple things as I report — could see me now, trying to get this distracted gum-chewing teenager to understand that unless she helps me, *I cannot do it.*)

My child wanders around through the pristine Easter patent leathers, the imitation Doc Martens, choosing finally a high-heeled, studded, tarty boot that some pervert has made for a child. "Will you please help her find something right for her age?" I beg the exhausted-looking girl, who probably has two other jobs. And what can my child be learning about adult self-sufficiency, or maternal protection, when I need to ask for help everywhere we go? I watch her delight, though, at what she considers the singular beauty of the cheap white leather shoes from Taiwan she has chosen. It is a moment of absolute happiness, to be out in the world with her, getting and spending, watching her do things outside the confining house. "Mommy, do you like these?" she asks.

And what did she feel?

She looks at me gratefully, almost reverently, because for many years we could not shop together, because I haven't ever taken her to a shoe store, and she is happy. I'm a consumer today, one who pays for goods. I'm a mother with a physical, practical *function*. There's a shine on us, a pride that we did it, and I bask in the light of our proper positions: I, the provider, I the driver, she the passenger, she the provided-for. Later, for a while, as I chop vegetables for dinner lying down, cheek to cheek with the onions, I am briefly at peace, not anguished by what all this is doing to her. She has a mother who served her. Bless the shoe store, bless the car that took me to the shoe store, bless parking spaces. Bless her feet, bless Taiwanese shoes and the salesgirl thereof. Bless shoes and boots made for walking, even if I can't, for very far.

And what happens later?

Later that day I realize that by purchasing those shoes, I may also have bought new physical pain, because what gives me pleasure — movement into the world, exposure, providing, being active not passive, being out in a store with my dazzling and dazzled daughter, myself overcome by the whirling display of goods — all this moving around will give me physical distress, then more subsequent sensory deprivation, for I will end up indoors again, for days. For relief, I will be horizontal again, the one who watches the child be delivered places by others, the woman at the window waiting for the child's return, the woman separated from the glimmering walking world outside.

That night, I dream I finally fall apart, what people have expected for a long time, and it's a too bright distorted dream. In my dream breakdown, memory of how to do things breaks first: I no longer know how to eat, how to tie shoes, how to count, spell, or move. So absolute is this *dumbness* of the body, body without central body-intelligence, the air itself becomes a kind of tangled forest that slows and stops me. Duties and skills and any exact "intuitions" of the body have stopped. I am lost and displaced in my own self.

For in the reality of these years, I have become a shadow woman who does a shadowy one tenth of what she used to do: procuring, loving, running from danger, helping, walking toward joy, shopping, entertaining, working. In my dream, even the shadow was gone, things I still do had disappeared, so that I was effaced, physiologically gone. In the strobing half-life of that dream, I was also remembering that I just got a new bottle of pills, and that the amber vial is a possibility. In the dream, that is. I pay for her beautiful shoes — and the ineluctable pleasure — with this dream.

I am awake for most of the night, seeing my life as a long inability that might last beyond these years, and that all the *unables* pin me like a moth waiting for ether. But those shoes are there in my daughter's room, like household gods protecting me in my flawed intactness, in my will to persist for her, despite my rage, despite the shadow woman who walks like the Tin Man when she walks at all.

My daughter wakes up, the house begins its noisy churning labor toward everyday life. When I make lunch, I praise myself for performing these daily chores, these tender mercies. The computer-programmed church bells peal down the streets over the town with "Love Lifted Me," the hymn of old-fashioned in-the-heart-and-gut salvation.

The Phantom of Compassion:
A Fairy-Tale Mélange

> True compassion is fraternal and sororal and not
> paternal, patriarchal or parental.
>
> — *Matthew Fox*

Once upon a time in the city, two women decided to enter the
hectic noise and glowing schmaltz of a popular musical. Both
knew what an adventure it would be; they were experienced ex-
plorers of the conventional world outside their forest, the one
with her white webbed lawn chair (call her Summerlie, for she-
who-lies-down-for-many-summers) and the other, now named
Lady Abundance, large and beautiful, accompanied by an also
large and indispensable wheelchair. Every creature in their
forest exclaimed, How wonderful you are, how brave. (Why
brave? they questioned.) But from years of going beyond the
familiar botany and soothing equipment of their environs, they

knew the "adventure" would be more full of unexpected twists and turns than anyone could want, ever.

Midafternoon, they set out in deep heat for the cool theater, having called for tickets many weeks before, and having paid dearly to behold the ornate spectacle. One strange thing: someone had called yesterday to ask if they knew they were in the Deaf Section? No, just the plain "disabled" zone, that's what we want, answered Summerlie. But she did wonder: Do all phone requests become part of the Central Confusion of General Disability? Had she not been completely clear about two "handicapped" seats in the best area?

While a kind man now helps Lady Abundance with her cumbrous wheelchair-unloading device, then pushing her inside, Summerlie waits. (The insurance company still considers a new electric wheelchair too luxurious, this one not difficult enough to get around in.) When Summerlie reaches the long line for picking up tickets, a dark cloud falls over her, for it is beginning — the real adventure — with its strange creatures and strange thorny paths. There is nowhere to sit *near* the line, therefore no way to wait *in* the line. However, there is a stone bench far across the lobby. What should she do? The white chair, though as faithful and reliable as a dog, cannot hold a place for her. But no matter: an officially instructed Princess Charming sees her dilemma, tells her to go to the front of the line. And suddenly the air flutters a little with awakened emotion. The people behind Summerlie become angry, like animals, barking with their narrowed eyes: Why is *she* cutting in? (Her cane has been forgotten in the car, the "telling-the-story" cane that never reliably works anyway, but does stop some from wondering.) As usual, she puzzles over what incites them so, what darkest magic makes these people begin to resemble wolves, as though in a fairy tale. Yet there is no little red hood in sight, all vulnerable and sad-looking, and in no way is Summerlie deceived — like that other girl in the forest — by these creatures whom she herself has grown to accommodate by labeling, if reluctantly, wolves.

Lady Abundance arrives with some strangers who have pushed the heavy wheelchair all the way into the marble lobby. Their open faces glow with good deeds and their own sense of generosity. For this, the two women are truly thankful, and they proceed down the corridors, below all the gold rococo and baroque seraphim and cherubim, all beautiful in their promise of a pure aesthetic romp in theater. Above is an eternal innocence, and down below is mortal complexity and misunderstanding.

They are an odd procession and know it: the summer chair is Day in all the velvet nightliness of the theater. It is like a pet out of place — at home domesticated and usual, part of the decor, but here unruly, as though it might lurch suddenly, embarrassingly out of control. The big wheelchair also disrupts the almost miniaturized elegance of theatergoers, disrupts their uncluttered view of the stage. No one wants this little surprise of strangeness before the grand one. But Summerlie and Lady Abundance know that stares and resentment lurk outside the ferny forest canopy of home and already adapted families and friends, so it is very difficult to venture out — at first so thrilling, a New World away from institutionalized comfort. They know that every time they disturb the universe in small ways, as T. S. Eliot has said. For a pleasing conformity and predictability of appearance is the real current of the American mainstream, and difference *disturbs*, whether it is this scene, or a couple with a different-colored adopted child, an amputee, a same-sex couple, an older woman with a young man.

When the ushers come to them — the women have asked again for their seats, disturbingly — they are all protest and objection in their white gloves and uniforms. "That wheelchair won't fit in the seating area." (But the women *paid*.) "What's that white chair, that *thing?*" (Takes up no more space than a wheelchair.) And, "I'll have to get my supervisor. I've never dealt with *that* before." (Which *that?* The Summerlie factor or the white-chair factor? Or the big wheelchair?) And before the women's eyes, the ushers too become like wolves, the cowering weaker kind who hide behind rules and defer to more powerful judgment. Who can blame them? Their salaries depend on this deference. But they are wolves nonetheless, unable to consider expanded definitions of "disabled," or to listen to the patient explanation of the chair.

The supervisor never comes. The ushers insist they cannot, will not, seat them without the supervisor. Five minutes before curtain, Summerlie and Lady Abundance are sent to the extreme side of the purchased seats, right up against the wall, and there they sit and recline, blocked from two thirds of each scene, knowing that people are glancing nervously at them. For there *will* be a ruckus over not being seated, and being treated like an assemblage of odd equipment and irritating human needs that no one wants to address. Why no one will take responsibility for seating these "unconventionals" in their proper, expensive seats *will* be addressed.

There had better be some big glowing stones to find our way out of this mess, Summerlie thinks. But they are not Hansel and Gretel, these two: they are adult and seasoned with the harsh pepper of dealing with the wolf-like for years. They are not lost, as some around them seem to be, in smugness and the not so hidden fear of affliction. They want to have a good time. Want their seats, want some wisp of courtesy. Do the ushers know only one category of injured or crippled or "differently abled"? For that matter, does the general public accept only a certain brand of crazy or disabled or blind or homeless as a kind of common stereotype — and find the others out of type, just plain odder? Just outrageous?

Lady Abundance knows they hate largeness: they would not stare if she were petite and unremarkable, with a petite and unremarkable chair. They have now been shunted aside, out of sight, and almost out of mind, in what the sociologist Philip Slater calls the Toilet Assumption — whatever society does not want to see, it tries to flush away, and that includes poverty, "imperfection," impediments of any kind, hunger, difference in sexual persuasion. Flush it: make them go away.

But these two are not flushable. *No more talk of darkness,* they hear from the stage. *Forget the wide-eyed fears.* But the real darkness is this: always the fear of being ostracized, like the phantom who hides in the dank forest of his basement. But these women still fight this particular discrimination, though Summerlie becomes exhausted because she's new to it and still all fisticuffs. For years Lady Abundance has been her own advocate, but she carefully chooses what issue to combat, then rests in acceptance, like crop rotation. Fight/grow, rest/fallow: crop of anger, crop of calm.

Until intermission, they hear the swollen themes of hiddenness, disfigurement, masquerade, and most of all, love and revulsion, all sung through the overripe score. The white-masked phantom begs for people to feel for the man behind the mask, but the pulpy music of the night is barely heard through the throbbing of anger in those two exiled so conspicuously to the side. Summerlie dares to wonder, though she is loath to compare: Is this what blacks feel in an all-white crowd? The obviously unemployed person in a crowd of workers? Overexposed but "wanting to disappear," where to not be noticed would be heaven?

The chandelier crashes on the stage. The elusive supervisor never comes.

Approaching a stony usher, Summerlie says, "Can't you do anything for us? So we can take our seats? Can you help us? Get the supervisor?" His rudeness is exemplary: he cannot move from his place, he says. Is he glued there for eternity? *Purge your thoughts of the life you led before.* Yes, in that previous life, this usher may have welcomed a question from a woman without such a chair, but his behavior now is like the pack's and his narrowing eyes say, This is so odd that my life as an usher, with an usher's predictable problems, is at stake. He knows what physical limitation, handicaps, whatever, look like, and This White Chair Isn't It. Neither is the oversized wheelchair his kind of problem. So he isn't going to help. He doesn't understand these particular creatures from the forest and doesn't want to, a form of xenophobia. And while ignorance is sometimes disguised as cruelty, cruelty can masquerade as ignorance too. No compassion for him, no magnanimous understanding from him, even though this is his *job:* to help customers, not to treat them like lint on his just-pressed gabardine uniform. He seems to hate: in the Bible, *hate* means "a simple lack of compassion," and if this were a morality play, he'd be Hatred, but a silly, pretentious version. Yes, they decide, the real phantom here is the phantom of compassion and intelligence, nowhere to be found this afternoon — no willingness to enter into the feeling of others in an awareness of mutuality and need.

Lady Abundance and Summerlie know that some are confused inside their involuntary wolf-hood: some have deep kindness in their DNA, empathy beneath the furs and pearls, and hidden in vest pockets. But the urge to accept is at war with some elemental repugnance, and that repugnance is what would send the two back home, or into the metaphorical recesses of the phantom's basement, where living in protected darkness might be easier than the harsh light of so much scrutiny. They fear the enervating comfort of the forest, but not more than this cultured peace, where eyes frisk them, and their sheer physicality is so much on display. Summerlie has had only eight years of disturbing a peace made of the usual, of learning how the toilet assumption operates on a minor scale, not to speak of the deeper disenfranchisement, for instance, of AIDS patients and others hidden away in hospices on quiet little streets.

Later, she decides to visit the wolf kings of this velvet desert, to advocate by telling the story of the most unlyrical, unfestive outing. But once there, how uncomfortable Summerlie feels in the manager's office, with the chair clashing like white patent leather in the classy dark winter of the air-conditioned office. She starts to talk, but how depleting advocacy often is, as though it leeches moisture from the very heartwood of living, to explain over and over the same thing, which is simply: accept and when necessary, adapt and provide what is humane and eases function, the bare bones of the Americans with Disabilities Act and justice in general. She explains the chair's use and describes the odd injury. What is never discussed even *in* the forest is the exhaustion of this kind of self-defense, the humiliation of delineating the body's malfunction to strangers. "Yes, it is a lawn chair. Without it I can't go anywhere because I cannot sit up." And does the staff know only about "normal-sized" wheelchairs? Why couldn't they have tried to fit it in the designated area? Does disability come in a few known shapes and sizes for them, with a few known appliances? She asks, "Does your staff know only canes and crutches?" What would they do with Tourette's syndrome, or people who must lie down on gurneys to go anywhere, or people with cervical cages who obstruct others' views? And what about a group of Martian transvestites in purple jumpsuits and sequined oxygen tanks?

Summerlie is done, and aches for the cool intimacy of the forest. One wolf promises a refund, not her goal: besides, they watched one third of the show, so two thirds back will be fine. It is promised. (It never arrives.) Conversation over. A teenage usher offers to help with the chair, and as they move awkwardly down the leviathan corridor, she turns around suddenly on intuition: the three skeptical wolves are watching her walk, as if to see if this really is a person with limited walking. Does she walk "disabled" enough for them to make her story believable? Do they think Summerlie is some twisted individual with a scam to get money back with a sob story? This, she decides, is also a form of mild "hate," what Graham Greene called a "failure of imagination," an inability to image up another's dilemma. She actually blushes to think these stooges doubt a story of such complexity with such embarrassing difficulty in the telling. To be watched like this is a violation: *No more talk of darkness,* indeed. They are creating more of it, watching her to see if she suddenly, fraudulently, might leap and run. Never again out like this, she vows. However, Lady Abundance will go again because she knows which darkness to let in just a little (like a homeopathic remedy, a little chases the rest away) and which to slam the door against. The well-broadcast claim is that this place offers good service — with élan too — to disabled persons, or persons differently abled, or ... Up close, the authentic caring is in the basement with spiders and mildew and no dewy music.

So Summerlie waits beside her chair while Lady Abundance negotiates the wheelchair, wheelchair loader, and car. Her eyes refuse to meet anyone else's: no more contact today with others' assessment of the impropriety of the white chair. But there's no peace in sight; an older man with a crew cut and blue blazer whistles up long enough to say, "How about that? You ready for a day at the beach?" Go away, all bringers of darkness. You dumb crew-cut wolf, you human being being stupid: go away, away, away.

But what does all this interior fury do? What does it do to Summerlie, transforming these people into animals? There is no superiority in categorizing them so: she doesn't enjoy name-calling, and she doesn't exactly hate them. More, it's as though the interminable *managing* occupies the space where patience and good humor lived before. In the musical, a character had said, "You'll learn to see the man behind the monster." But she wonders if she can still see the people behind the wolves. Someone also tells the phantom that his soul is disfigured, not his body. Is she losing herself to the disfigurement of constantly angry perceptions? Probably not. She and Lady Abundance have intact and lively souls that are simply bruised from the steady pressure of scrutiny and subtle prejudice.

They drive home through hot traffic to the compassionate forest of their familiars. Lady Abundance talks about the early morning: how beautiful it was today, how she couldn't cross the room to the alarm clock without banging pain. Summerlie is hungry, but there's no handicapped parking for Abundance in front of the chosen restaurant. They plan to go swimming next week, a chore and a graceful, redeeming thing at once. Summerlie starts preparing herself for *her* masquerade because so often entering the house after an adventure with stories of outrage is bad for all. Yet it is always so: starting out hopeful, coming back freshly slapped, disillusioned almost every time. First she talks of the wild music, the wonderful costumes, the scale and noise, and then she goes upstairs to cry. What happened to Caritas, charity? To authentic, felt apology? Those powerful wolf-like creatures with smooth voices, and lofty community goals, cannot truly imagine another person's dilemma.

Whenever that music comes on in the future, she will ask that it be shut off. For the music becomes a deep reflecting pool, and in it she sees the two of them, and many others, try and fail, fail and rise again simply to try the pleasures of an outside world without fanfare or commotion, a world completely and seamlessly available before. *Purge your thoughts of the life you led before.*

And later when Summerlie has the vigor to write a letter in protest, back comes such heavy condescension that it is amazing it doesn't sink to the bottom of the mail pile: "We understand this was a difficult afternoon for you." (Who is *this* person behind the stiff mask, to interpret what they experienced as *mere difficulty?* "The staff all were dismayed." (Translation: pissed off at the bizarro white chair.) "Their actions were successful." Successful because no fist fights? And behind the spat-out, word-processed letter, what attitudes are hidden? What self-deception? True, some few were civil: but what was paid for was never got, and what was hoped for — a smooth evening —

crashed down like the chandelier. And what was lost for Summerlie in the darkness and in the too brilliant stage light was the confidence to leave the forest any time soon. There at least it was possible to live somewhat happily, if also confined. She became quite busy making her part of the forest even more beautiful than before, tucking herself in. However, they will both ask ever after, why the phantom of compassion and fairness is so often locked away in the depths of the human basement.

Moonswimming

You who were darkness warmed my flesh
. . . O node and focus of the world . . .
— *from "Woman to Child," Judith Wright*

We are standing in water that looks like jittery black oil this late
at night, late July bulging with heat in Windham, Maine. How
can we let them do this, those almost invisible yet glowing children out there, diving from black into black? Because it's so
hot: we're all steaming.

Adults are scattered all around like sentinels; some by the
shore, some by the diving float, some closer in, knee-deep in
the shallower water. Where the moon hits the water, it becomes
opalescent, seems to swim there, the water then swimming
through the children's limbs, after they dive into the molten
core at the end of the pier.

Where is *my* child?

I am one of the watchers, the keepers of the vigil, just like any other parent — *not* in the background now, *not* growing less capable each year. I am becoming usual, mainstream, finally conjoined in duties with the other parents here, who for years watched me recline at the edge of the "paintings" of recreational life at this small vacation place. Does my daughter notice I am here if she needs me? Here I am helping along with the others — the worriers, the calmers of the worriers, the tipsy nonchalant men, the men and women who are here *with me* in the water, instead of helping me stand or setting up my chair.

The children jump off the board in silhouettes perfectly cut, seeming far away as they break into the slick night element. We stagger their turns at diving with warning and reprimand. *Wait 'til he's out. Now go,* or *Not now, calm down and wait.* If one child were to land on top of the other in the flawed, shifting perspective of night . . . well, we can't even think of it, so we keep inspecting the water (as with a jeweler's loupe) and keep barking out the orders. *Wait, wait.* And they are safe for now; we know their growing heads are full of gold and mischief and every hope, that the intelligence is like liquid sapphires, and one small mistake could ruin all the riches.

It is dangerous and I am letting my daughter do it. Attention, attention! Please note: your mother is one of the ones *standing* here, in charge, poised to help, somewhat powerful — Mother Courage, Powerful Mother, not lying-down mother, no longer Mother Cannot. Over and over, the missiles of their bodies aim for that moon at the end of the diving board, and they scream their success. *I did it, and I couldn't last year. Cool,* the younger ones say.

Look at all of us, middle-aged and mostly aimed for caution, for the serious goal, aimed for bankruptcy, for success, for failing health or longevity, recovering from depression or plunging into it, happy, mournful — each aimed toward what is unknown. But we are strangely quiet, knee-deep in sleepy reverie, connected by invisible threads to the one or two children out there in the Grand Canyon of water, then each of us wakening instantly every time the water breaks with another crackling dive.

Purposeful and brave, we are also conventional. In a tribal way, we are simply keeping watch over each other's children, while we are wired like armatures to our own. But for me, standing up to guard is a renaissance. My daughter twists, hits the water, turns, she goes under, then breaches, skinny and iridescent in her perfect skin, her whole animal self winking like a diamond in the onyx setting of the lake, the *fade-proof lake*. *Great job*, I say, meaning, *Can we go now?* and *Don't swim at night without me ever. Take me along always.*

For maternity is obdurate, relentless, adamantine. If compromised in some physical or emotional way, recovering it partially is one face of bliss; for me it is being here, guarding; for others winning custody, or being released from a hospital, or learning to diaper with one hand. There she is diving alone again, her hair phosphorescent, and she is tall and long. (I used to think that when I became upright, she'd still be young enough for me to experience again the important warmth of carrying her, that time would twist itself beneficently around us; she still the size of three or four, me forty-nine, my present age, so that I could pick her up again, she who has not been picked up by her mother in eight years.) But, no, she is almost five feet tall. She dives alone again into the epicenter of the moon in the middle of the lake in the middle of my life.

PART FOUR

WOMAN IN A
WALKING GARDEN

Elixir

There were the roses, in the rain.
Don't cut them, I pleaded.
      They won't last, she said.
But they're so beautiful
      where they are.
Agh, we were all beautiful once, she
      said,
and cut them and gave them to me
in my hand.

          — *"The Act," William Carlos Williams*

As I walk, hunched over with a cane but up in the world, I see rosebushes attached to almost every lawn and porch railing — unremarkable, scruffy, plain red. Six more houses with more rosebushes until I reach the office for another appointment, conscripted by myself to *talking it out,* nineties-style, when what is really necessary is body renovation. Little serenity will happen until I am at ease in the world of mobility, where I can trust my body not to alienate me and can achieve a sense of belonging to it, recapturing it. I am trying to heal the fractures accumulated in a fall from grace, falling to positions of misalignment and loss of place.

I, who have never grown a single weed or plant, suburban-grown but city-bound, grew an obsession in the complex soil of discontent and exile. Too much unremitting solitude becomes like a prison, as it is for shut-ins, and some confined by illness or agoraphobia. Prisoners decorate their cells, become born-agains, let the neurotic or creative seeds bloom and grow.

But even solitude can sometimes grow *something,* a crop of rituals to make it through the daunting *everydayness,* whether it's endless television, solitaire, or compulsive cooking: you become like a human strobe, lighting one subject too much. In these acres of intractable privacy — interrupted by friends who seemed like aliens because they could move through different seemingly astral worlds in one day — I grew imaginary roses, obsessed by a beauty I once considered frivolous.

A rose, any rose, is a destination without a journey, a Zenness. Up close, eye and nose to fleshy petal, roses seem to have a soulfulness, and a quiet room can appear crowded with their intensity. Is it only confined people, and those famished for stimuli, who become this focused? But view the inward radiance, like a light inside a cave —the cave the analogue for the deep-colored throat nearest the calyx, pronged like a setting that holds the fat, then tapered, jewel of flower. Roses have a withheld mystery, an attar, an *inglowing:* Would the Sterling Silver rose rather be pewter? White Dorothy, who are you? Rose Brawardine: elegant, aristocratic? Evangeline, "indistinct in twilight"? Sometimes you want to explore a rose before the sun or water does, and by intuitive touch force out the secret of the fertile flower that is "organ," fecund with complexity: stamen, pistil, corolla. (There is even a rose called exotic Rubaiyat. What passionate story lies within that naming?)

The obsession grew. I was inside too much, spinning tales through miles of interior gardens. (Others might decide the TV is hypnotic and full of truth; the weather too fascinating for words; the phone too magically and hurtfully quiet; the bourbon so mysteriously shrinking in the bottle.) My reclusive grandmother studied every aspect of Lawrence Welk, every tree outside her window, every delivered cut of meat, every neighbor. How could I be leading her elderly life?

But, confined or not, look at the faces of opening roses, and you can see the untouched cheeks of babies, goddesses, Moses in the bulrushes. As the flowers keep blooming, the plot thickens, and the perfect symmetry collapses, with petals widening out to mother-air, then unpredictably closing like an older child with secret dreams and a hidden code of growth. Then they droop, they loosen rebelliously, they are no longer immaculate. They have achieved a fine wildness. Afterward, their most intense color spilled, the muscles in the petals weaken and fall. Naturally I have empathy for this new fragility after so much energy.

So much vitality everywhere this fall, the *inglowing* of roses, mixed with all the melancholy and fade: Sienna and cadmium petals, like ghostprints of leaves, leaves the sister of petals.

The roses are blooming in loose family clusters: brown leaves and rusty leaflets, runt roses and renegade roses, big Mother roses, and wildly branching outlaw roses, worm-bitten roses, the shy ones, the ones malformed and dusted with fertilizer, the I'm-More-Beautiful-Than-You-Are rose. All attach to the family bush, the ragged, unbeautiful compound, with beautiful room for everyone, even the unbudded, even the one that shakes too much in the wind, even the one almost gone entirely, with just one petal left, which the fall breeze would like to blow off, but the family won't allow it. It's a kinetic but solid configuration; what I love is the blooming together, the self-love of roses.

There's a text in these bushes that keeps the flawed, the overstated, the ugly, the gone-past-bloom, by holding them together within the system of leggy branch and root and nurturing acid soil. No self-pruning, no leaving behind and no impatience to slough off the less than perfect.

And when I read about people building a garden together, I assume too romantically that they are happy together, as fiercely attached as the rosebushes. (Is anyone else familiar with the melancholy force-bloomed in those moments before a therapy appointment? The pitch? The volume? With the way an imagined perfect family can materialize?) See *that* mythical family all kneeling down together over there, evenly spacing the small bushes; the earth loam, the bits of shell and worm and root all feel the industrious press of their fingers, which accidentally and happily touch each other. They plan the mulching together, the protection from winter injury, especially injury.

Why are they looking up? To check the weather? Surely the weather between them is always good. Perhaps they are seeing if the early suburban dusk matches the color of the rose, Crepuscula, orange pink fading to apricot, as the light grows crepuscular, or is it the color of Rêve d'Or, dream of gold, or Sutter's Gold? Surely each person has a strong and functional body. There is no outsider in this airbrushed family, no non-performer who can't work, no one lying on the grass. No one to be left behind when they decide to go to somewhere to eat, or to buy more bushes, to take the children for a long walk. *(You don't mind, do you? Being alone for a few hours? Waiting in the back seat while we eat breakfast?)* No estrangement lives in this unreal family, no suspicion of malingering; no one with an awkward disability gets in the way.

The family disappears.

Disability is an inconvenience to others, slowing them down in their pursuit of easy exuberant fun. It's a litmus test of loyalty, testing forbearance in friendship and in intimate relationship because of delays, changed plans, extra work, unpredicted needs: Can you hand me that cane? Can you carry that chair for me? Does the restaurant have a bench so I can lie down? Could you please bring the car around? (One of my friends saw social invitations fall away that day she started using a heavy wheelchair.) On the part of the sufferer, it also creates a real desire to have the impatient others suffer too in *just the same way*, the engorging fantasy of revenge. (*You* just lie here in the heat while we walk to the pond. *You* don't mind, do you, if I just make you stay inside the house for three weeks?)

Those Crepuscula roses do not bloom. But I think of the old yellow rosebushes outside my parents' house in Ohio, and from that vision, I name some roses of my own, in the way people grow proprietary about naming flowers. Six years horizontal, of fading with conflict blooming in my garden, as complicated as roots, I say, like Adam naming the animals — You, light yellow one, shall be Loyalty Everlasting. And the hopeful pinks over by the Victorian house, Softness to Come; the creamy substantial whites, A Portion of Happiness; the sassy peach, Impudent Longing (for what's in the Rubaiyat); and the warm orange ones nearly growing in the concrete, Love Returning, Love Returning, repeated twice like a chant. And yes, that plump one, Body Blooming; the buttery yellow one in front of the psychiatrist's office, Hope without Edges. All of my varieties are resistant to disease, beetles, slings and arrows, the scissor and the knife. (Of course! of course!) They bloom everywhere, in every habitat, and last forever. I am walking through these streets, really walking, leaving behind those who left me, because of fear, or the inconvenience I was — clumsily in need, needily dependent at times.

Even at night they bloom. The insomniac notices the petals look like fallen moths swimming in a pool of light from the streetlamp. (Could these be White Wings? — I wish for those wings now, when I see wheelchairs, when I remember wanting wings for a wheelchair, to fly above the people's stares.)

Glorious Mundi: the autumn blooms with the ones I name, glory of the world and the walking in it thereof.

*

Agh, we were all beautiful once.

Some say that wistfully or doubtfully, as we age, trying to fill up the important space where youth or vigor lived with comfort and comforting, or with some bloom of also-aging love, loyalty or companionship. Some gratefully take the consolations of those cut blooms offered in that poem, not regretting the *temps perdu.* But some of us still clench our fists, refuse any propitiatory offering (spiritual or psychiatric or material), as if an important bone is broken in the receiving hand. We stand in the rain that still batters the roof over the rehab pool, or the wheelchair, or the counseling office where we spent so much time that is lost, regretting it and furious still. No, I can accept no consolation for all the years of not being *able* with my child, *unable* to work, *disabled* in marriage, friendship, work. That time of body-exile was like being in a tin shack, with stones thrown on it. When you're suddenly disabled, there's the regret stone (look at all I'm missing), the anger stone (why did this happen to me), the guilt stone (everyone is suffering because of me), the envy stone (how come everyone gets to go food shopping, to movies, to stores). I lay inside myself, bruised with the noise of self-pity and anomie. (And of all the emotions, self-pity is the one that healthy others find taboo. Anything but *that*. It's a friend-repellent.)

I'm walking now, but my *self* is still horizontal or being wheeled around, incapable of lasting solace, a stubborn soul that can't heal because of the lasting imprint of my experience. So, while the spirit is in some dark corner, not yielding, the body is outside this September, romping with the colors of fall. Half of the horizontal woman is upright and half is still on the floor, as though disability is like omnipresent phantom pain. Half up, half down, the woman might seem comical in a cartoon.

At a rehabilitation hospital, there is the gift of "support therapy," therapy that holds you up by its knowledgeable compassion and authentic fluency in the language of chronic pain, spoken by experts schooled in dealing with trauma. Later, sprung from that hospital, we are sent to more therapy by our intimates, who are impatient for the good old person to emerge from behind a swarm of cynicism or negativity, or from the black humor that is so very black and blue. In short, to recover, uncover, and discover our old selves within the wounded self-image that has taken over like root rot. *Come out, come out, wherever you are* . . . But the whole persona, subjected to the detached eye of medical scrutiny, pokes, CT scans, MRIs, interrogation and inquiry of hands — that person, even on the way to recovery, still has the broken-down body fossilized *inside* the new growth of getting better. The idea of the well-functioning, taken-for-granted-body is gone forever.

What does anyone suddenly traumatized with a long time coming back say to a shrink? *Who am I? Give me a new image of myself that includes the suffering but doesn't let it show on the surface? Give me my lost years back, and neutralize the bitterness. Help me throw the regret stone away.* For years, I was not seen as a woman; as a disabled friend, yes, as a mother with mobility problems, as a wife who needs help, yes, seen in that way. We need to be honest. Do you see the man first or his lost arm? The woman first or the wheelchair? The physical strength of that tall man or his unfocused blind eyes? I was a patient, mostly. *Tell me how to fix the effects of that unseenness, that state of neuterdom.* Patients are handled by professional probers; they start to feel like raw material. I barely recognized myself, the woman in the mirror, who had gained thirty, then forty pounds, from inactivity, stooped over, hair askew from lying down, slovenly, suspicious that everyone wonders, Can't she just take one more minute to make herself look better? (No, I couldn't. It was too hard to stand up.) Suddenly I had become *unbeautiful* to myself and felt that it spread wherever I went, to my mate, to a house grown ugly, to the hospital grown uglier. Even as I walk through the shocking leaves of yellow-brown and carmine, the smeared beauty on the pavement, I remember, dear doctors, the unbeautifulness.

Part of femaleness, but only part, is feeling an animal possibility, the elation of possibly attracting new sexual interest, with the potential of acting upon it, even if there's no real desire to carry through. With chronic pain, clumpy sneakers and a cane or wheelchair, erotic possibility felt canceled, or at least for me, and with that, my femaleness partly canceled too. No one seemed a possible lover because no one saw me that way. Not to be looked at longingly anymore; of course that is the hard truth of the past tense: *We were all beautiful once.* But in me the sense of lost attractiveness had been sped up. Stolen were those accidental glances from strangers that as contemporary women we are not supposed to want . . .

I am getting into a car, quite a spectacle in itself: cane thrown in first and body "bent" as much as possible to get in the back door, lying on the mattress the goal. But before that, a dignified, unusually handsome older man looks over in my direction; will the glance smolder or deepen? I hope. Then I hear from his lovely plummy mouth, *Can I be of assistance to you?* End of the imagined sensual drama. I was not seen, except in terms of needing help. *Agh, we are not beautiful anymore. I am seen as an extension of my stupid cane, my shoes, my awkwardness, doctor.* I had been unsexed in my image of self, and no healer can (or should) "re-sex," exactly as no healer can truly revitalize the truly anemic spirit in a series of office appointments.

Teach me not to fear my unreliable body. Can you do that? Outside the office, the leaves blow around in the silvery September wind, leaves and petals in an identical sun-burnt red, all of it as moist and odorous as an old bear's habitat. *Unteach us this truth: some people just give up on you.* The rose petals in the rain are swept away. The cars hiss by. Fragrant Cloud, Golden Wings, Old Smoothie, High Noon. The sweet names soothe. Glorious Mundi.

Leaving the house of hard healing, I walk carefully on my own two feet, my feet pressing an odd wine out of the compost on the sidewalk. The next autumn rose sighted will be named Glorious Mobile: *glorious to move, to be moving.* I am not locked in a house; I am not in a wheelchair, making skinny tracks through the mulch: I am walking, gloriously, and the splintered spirit will catch up.

Everything is drenched in deep color, as though torn from a Fra Angelico fresco, where the figures appear to be caught off guard, but ready for the accidental color of deliverance. I will memorize this illuminated page of fall, as I memorized the text and subtext of roses.

They are so beautiful where they are.

My feet are beautiful where *they* are.

Pastoral

What men or gods are these . . .
What mad pursuit? What struggle to escape? . . .
What wild ecstasy?

— from "Ode on a Grecian Urn," John Keats

Under the burnt-auburn copper beech tree, a student is reciting
a poem of loss and sweet conventional longing. Many Japanese
parents and German tourists pass by, many rambunctious students and janitors and Saturday-drifting faculty. Office hours
are being held here, under the tree, with the teacher obviously
instructing from the white recliner and the student obviously
performing in the old-fashioned way of large inflection and exaggerated rhythm, all the lawn's deep greens before them, so
tropical they hardly belong on a sedate university lawn.

Later I will know that my student (which sounds proprietary but could not be less so) resembles my father, with his

unexceptional light skin, eyes a wishful but flat blue, and reddish hair a few shades darker than the tree's unearthly color.
His body is as square and solid as a wrestler's. His clean good
looks could make him a poster kid for army recruitment: *We
need you now.*

*Fair youth, beneath the trees, thou canst not leave thy song, nor
ever can those trees be bare* . . . Keats would say.

Fair youth: I need him. *Lay your sleeping head, my love,
human on my faithless arm* . . . Now Auden just barged in on this
untimely, indecorous summer dreaming. Wait. That's only my
student there, only a person enrolled in a summer class, not a
sleeping, loving anyone. But fragments of poems fly in and out
of my head in the summer like streamers, like tides, like fish in
an aquarium, like similes.

In conference, when his hands are close to mine, plain peasant hands near my plain peasant hands, they seem irresistible.
Both sets count the iambics, as both minds mull over the word
that dovetails perfectly for the well-carpentered line. (Listen to
this unseemly rhapsody.) Irresistible because so vulnerable, and
in need of care: hands almost touching, but definitely, ethically,
emphatically not. No wild ecstasy. And those hands usually
shake with the drugs he takes for multiple addictions. Together,
we could be seen and imagined as if from a great aesthetic, even
aerial distance, a new frieze on a contemporary Grecian urn:
the strangely placed woman, the student with a shaft of gleam-
ing hair, and at the side a third figure, Imagination the Conjurer, who invents these stories of unrequitedness, and the
chase and the ever after. The fourth, the tightly robed Code en-
forcer, who has more steady power than the others, presides.

But now the student is speaking of lighthouses in the real,
not invented summer, reciting his poem grandly, as though

under an invisible spotlight, under a tree that seems now to have turned the surprising color of his hair. Clearly, this man twenty-five years younger than I performs just for me, staring up at each dramatically emphasized line break. At once all excess and unreason, I am moved to regret all the life led without him; I have missed him, without knowing him, for forty-seven years, though there is much of bright interest and goodness in my own life. But why? The regret implodes: the answer is one of the oldest stories, pounding today like a headache that might last, not like any recognizable joy. This is what I want, this is what I cannot have. He's the unchased youth on the old urn, and I am older than my age.

Gratefully, there are sensible rules about why people cannot go beyond the borders of designated roles, though of course many do trespass. That's the strict code: *No mad pursuit.* Then there is the heart's seething hidden code, and Shakespeare's code about the irrelevance of age, for "Thou hast nor youth nor age; / But, as it were, an after-dinner's sleep, / Dreaming on both." But who's dreaming? Who's sleeping? Don't we all feel age as a trip wire, or a blessing, more acutely in summer? Unblessed, I'm too wide awake, with a poem before me that needs improvement, needs me, though his work is far more skilled and daring than mine at the same age. He has been forced out of youth too early, exposed to strange love and trouble, this young man perfectly physically formed, with his own disabling anguish. Objectified on the urn, he would be Vigor, and she the draped figure who thinks herself not lovely, and odd because she cannot sit up for a conference, and what strange hunched walking! When she walks like an elder, with a despicable cane, she has gone way past her real age. But he, vibrant outside, but wounded inside, must see her first as strangely "disabled," as a older teacher secondly, and third, as a woman — and all three not very gracefully braided together. If he knew the yearning, would it be grotesque to him? But on this urn, in this warm pastoral, no one knows what anyone else feels, whether anyone dreams of youth or age.

So I do not have that after-dinner's sleep, dreaming of both, with a nice old brandy and a silk dinner jacket. I am slammed awake by rules, blunt self-appraisal, unbidden lyrics that will never appear on any contemporary urn: For ever wilt thou love, and he be fair. Forever will he be reading in the green pastoral, forever will I be reclining through those years of formal teaching in the most casual of poses. Forever will the young be yearned for, the old be not . . . Forever wilt thou remember, and he forget, muses the midsummer mind, drunk with lines wandering in from here and there, to stanch longing or create it.

In front of us is the bulky Henry Moore sculpture, a green-gold Amazonian beauty full of holes and exotic molten curves that open wide and settle hard in the life of the onlooker. Laps of tyrants and mothers are in the piece, and fierce attachments; the lover's elongated demanding hip, the crotches of olive trees; open spaces we wish we had *cleaved unto;* angles of remorse that jab, like poor decisions, near a breastlike curve; here and there a foothill of defeat, or beginnings. Places to get lost, places we are found; homelike, meadowlike, expansive, claustrophobic in uterine association. I listen to his poem, stare at the statue: he is tender to the quavering places in his own work, oblivious to the dreamy middle-aging of his listener. The tourists stare at him, at us, at the bulkiness of Moore's own aesthetic longing. O youth surging in the green shoots of new poetry, O mid-age woman, a solid mass in a new double aging, with physical limitations that have unloved the body, with the real sensuality now the exquisite lack of pain on some days. This is the authentic old story: not Auden's heat and pleading, not Keats's fever, not Shakespeare's after-dinner's sleep. My story . . .

*

Q: So what do you want, person about to slide off the Grecian urn with yearning? What is it, this envy, *this* desperation?

A: I want to get out of this reclining chair and stay out of it, be the standing, running figure on the urn, be who I was, before this, before him.

*

And to heal him, in the way that I have needed healing; to plant, then harvest, a serenity as steady as the delft blue of the sky above the copper coinage of the tree. I can hear, just as though it were Brahms, the swell of his own mental suffering, perhaps because it's an honored tradition in our family also, generation after generation. About mine, he knows (rightfully) little except for a the story of the chair that explains a reclining teacher and is for some the bridge to their own islands of psychic or physical difference. But there is a rhythmic current between us that breaks against the closed octaves of solitude: we are knowing here, *cleaving unto* in this summer pastoral.

And how would you heal? Old Teacher, Youngish Woman, the figure now falling into the arms of the Conjurer — the Conjurer who loves high drama and plots without brakes or earthboundedness . . .

I would draw him into my more cultivated field, teach him how to seed and plow and harvest all his *words* — an endeavor far from sexual — but partaking of heat as strong as the sun's. For him I would absorb the destructive years, and the months in addiction centers, that hide like marrow in the poems. And absorb all this into my stronger self, larger because it has been elongated by time and different trouble that has brought me close to where he has been — close to lostness. But now he is my figure on the urn, my unknowing, unpiped youth, blind to my desires — desires more like a healer's than a teacher's or a lover's, all stirred together, and also stirring. For this is an almost maternal longing for nurturing him and does not exact anything at all. But I will not emerge from this pastoral occupying the same place in the landscape. Because he is the light that fell on the green field of the lawn but darkened it by exposing me to visceral new knowledge: that my youth is not the greatest *gone,* though it has been wrenched away too soon. Graceful mobility, a drawing scent of confident self is more gone, *gone and gone.* He would disdain the passionate, imagined affinity not merely because of age — but because the woman in front of him is odd, *weird, far out,* whatever word his usually beneficent vocabulary would find.

The hour is over.

The singular performance is almost over. Still there is longing, and the longing for detachment from this iridescence — a paradox more easily articulated than lived with. He will brave his talented way through his life. Brave, unhappy youth, all you need to know is healing, which you yourself must harvest, and are harvesting in words and in perseverance, steadying your jumping hands. Wild ecstasy you have and can use.

And now, as if to punctuate resolve, the automatic sprinkler system flashes like foil raining up from the hidden spigots, like sudden clarity. The new smell of water on hot grass blends with the Gauloise smoke of the French students, along with a heavy odor of fertilizer. We are so surprised we laugh, and the fire of all this imagining is drenched by water, soaking papers, soaking him, the solid body heat of the sculpture, suffused with all our Rorschachs in the summer sun. He runs to the next event. Forever will he run, and she be watching. For we have youth and age and certain damage, and will someday learn a kind of after-dinner's sleep, for calming. Conference over again.

There Goes Your Other Life

> Optimistic and realistic planning of family outings
> and activities demonstrates that the family can func-
> tion as before.
>
> — Building a New Dream,
> *Janet R. Maurer and Patricia D. Strasberg*

The family outing: they went, I waited.

The spring river swelled in the rain and the birds were
eerily quiet. When my family started up the hill to hike Pink-
ham Notch, I couldn't be with them; I will not ever be with
them for any steep, long climb. But the jealousy was no longer
the same about the inflated thrill of these outings, and the way I
imagined that communion deepened during such invigorating
activities. Two people walking away from me now had become, roughly, two people walking away to an adventure —
no longer exclusion, or the trigger for an angry emptiness.

Not swamped by yearning, I could find interest elsewhere, in the ecstatic recreation of plain walking itself, considering what happens to a family when its kaleidoscopic composition abruptly changes and stays changed.

Staying back was not always easy, and it is not true that a family ever "can function as before," merrily rolling along, after sudden serious injury, new disability, or illness. That is a glib assumption, showing an absence of appreciation for family psyche and design — one that contributes to no one's welfare. Why do experts insist on giving a pretty rainbow of false assurances?

Someone falls out of the design. The kaleidoscope turns, and so does the whole function and emotional pattern embedded in it. For a while randomness reigns; there are just particles aching to belong somewhere without turbulence. Father, mother, child — falling and searching for stability. Three equaled three once, but then what in our house? The math was different. Two ate dinner in one room, one lay down in the next room; and two went everywhere, one stayed behind. Two got on with the high jinks of living, one was static and remote. Later it changes.

*

From a diary entry of years ago, there is the raving expletive of a woman forsaken: "So, I cannot walk to Pilgrim Heights. So, look at the ocean from here. So look at the light through the windows. I can't believe I wrote about this fucking beautiful place and I can't walk to it. Sick of cannot, hate cannot. Aren't there any beaches without boardwalks . . . Leave it to us to buy a crappy portable wheelchair that can't even make it over the bumps."

Et cetera: a longing, vulgar woman fed up with being trapped in the car, or perhaps on the ground with the ants and the imagined ticks. A woman who believes she won't ever walk a whole block, much less down this long boardwalk to Pilgrim Heights, hates the fact of presciently writing years before about the body smoothly absorbed away into this incomparable ocean beauty. The body was then just a body, an admirer, an intimate. What did she know of physical transformation? *There go the feet of your usual body, your hands / your stiffly seeing eye / there goes your other life,* went the poem. The coordination of legs went, the hands didn't, the eye quickened in its socket with needing to see and compute things anew. Three minus one equaled two, two spinning off, one piece left behind. A particular woman, yes, with a particular physical problem, but a woman generic in sharing with many others an isolating apartness. There are those on the sidelines who cannot benefit from the fool's promise of "optimistic and realistic planning" — while the walkers just walk away (and probably those same sideliners break the textbook expectations of persevering goodness and calm acceptance by often being not at all Adapted or Adaptable). But there she was, I was, newly alone; many at the rehabilitation hospital were more debilitated, far more alienated, but all were in a vortex of catastrophic change, bodies and families squeezing into a new form that would never function as before. Anyone would be shocked at new exclusion, while others dance away, drive away, fun away, as they must in order to have spacious normal lives, which I encouraged. But when they did disappear around the bend, to the mall or dinner or sledding or the movies, the anger flared double, like fire in August.

There goes the other life . . . two people down a simple path just because they want to, because the path is smooth and the ocean is there, like a rippling orchard — for those who stand close by the edge. That was our landscape: a wide everything with the two in it, a narrowing down to me. There was no guide for how to behave when left behind. Bitterness remained but softened as I started to go out tentatively, go places with a cane.

*

I still can't walk all the way down that boardwalk, nor can I run or move with self-assurance or without fear. Still there is the longing for the extremes of wild kinetic experience that children love, which only one parent has provided for the whole of my daughter's young childhood, now gone forever. Even now, I do not always participate in everything I am capable of doing, whether from fatigue or fear of new injury, or because I'm saving up by banking the body for the next adventure.

But wanting to have those "wild" adventures is one category; another altogether is the fevered envy of alliances forged by sharing activities without me. The subsequent emotional exclusion has lasted, even as improvement occurs. Even when I could join again, a part whirling back into place, the design itself had changed on its own and would never be as before. I had been left out, by nature of the fact that motion runs the world, not stillness. Now I was trying to catch up, not just *being* or *doing*, and defensive about my lagging position.

For I had been dependent, I, who had won autonomy of spirit and selfhood at a price, and valued it deeply. Dependence erodes the structure of relationship. Horizontalism caused this dependence; dependence compromised my motherhood, and this was the big insult. For all the emotional protection I could offer — quiet time and expansive physical affection born from fierce love — there was much I could not do. But the maternal passion was there, with its great claws, ready to pounce if necessary. Many women have those claws, whether Masai or Appalachian or paraplegic or impoverished or shellacked society matrons. Although restricted, that capacity for defending still lives on but is more difficult, and so an angry frustration, mixed with the protective passion, boils dangerously. Still, one holds as tight as tape to what is possible, using imagination: off to the pediatrician I went, driven by a friend, then listening on the floor to medical instructions. And I was careful not to let my child feel responsibility for my welfare, or that she had to be good to keep things smooth. So when an arrogant young teacher once suggested that my kindergartner was being "parenticized," that is, taking the role of parenting the parent because I was disabled, the claws came out. In our house, no one was allowed to tell her to take care of her mother. *Her* happiness would not be eroded by any such reversal; our unspoken contract was not sullied. I cared for her in all the ways I could; she was in an odd safe nest, however different, with the Chair Elevator grinding up and down the stairs.

But for us the fact was that the power kept gathering in the physically powerful parent, and inevitably *this* imbalance ignites tempers, minimizes virtue, and makes a daily life already filled with bruising obstacles more difficult. Take a child's natural request to use the bathroom on one of these outings. The mother should take the young girl to the bathroom, across the circus space, but it is too far to walk. She is furious again for this so maternal a deprivation. So? Many mothers can't. Child "understands" because she has to. Can't this horizontal woman get it straight? Father will do it. Is the child embarrassed to go to the men's room, or to have him wait? Many children deal with this all their lives. Parents start bickering; the real source is the mother's disappointment, "role failure," as she might sarcastically see it, relying always on his legs, his exquisite ability, his surface cheerfulness. Powerful father "wins" again at child care, though no one wants him to, and father and child wander off to solve the logistics of bathrooms. She's there like a mannequin on the grass. Will the child trust him more later because he masters most of their world now?

A few years older, a few years later, the child knows her slowly getting-better mother loves big, sweeping Cape Cod, especially the lunar buff-colored dunes you can approach from the long boardwalk in Pilgrim Heights, sees her lying in the car, falsely smiling. She feels torn, perhaps. Should she stay with her mother? Mother knows the child's dilemma, hates that the child is burdened so. Father is tall and strong and takes the knowing child away, the child who now wants to go, of course. Is this a sunlit family reassuming its life easily? Is this the result of inadequate planning? Every outing is "off"; everything is lopsided and ill-fitting, despite the best intentions. Everyone always feels slightly nervous, not quite pleased or calm much of the time.

On a more practical level, regard the simple requirement, dinner: how preparing it refutes everything about a family's ability to be as it was before. In the first worst stage, the able, empowered parent chooses, fetches, cooks, and delivers to the hungry child and reclining dependent. The "dependent" rails. Why that brand of bread? Why not low-sodium soy sauce? Unfortunate that the capable one must do all this, but even with many offers of help, financial and culinary, preparation of food may be one way to achieve minor control over this new and troubling disarray.

Stage two: he gets the groceries, cooks the meal, but the formerly unable person now helps to clean up, in fact more and more *can* do things, but now the able-bodied one resists intrusion because a new pattern is in place, one in which the whole show is run one way.

Stage three: I stand long enough to prepare half the meal with food he has purchased, and of course I criticize his selections because they are not mine, and no matter how much we do battle over these minutiae, the battle is over loss of dominion. His exhaustion is fueled by too much confined bad time together. (Can't you get what I want? Chunky applesauce is better. Answer: I'm doing the shopping. Just be happy someone is doing the shopping.) Of course, we are like unsheathed nerves, as irritable with each other as with the medical world, the child in the middle like a spectator at some twisted emotional Olympics that fast become nagging, high-pitched. The child's head moves from side to side to see which accusation hits the other harder. And this is not uncommon in families where stress goes past 104 degrees in the shade.

Stage four: I do some shopping, I do some cooking, and I clean up. But in no way do we function as before, and not just because of battling and hermetically sealed togetherness. The transformation of one person into relative helplessness, and the other into the generous though often annoyed deliverer of services — into the Prince of Patience, according to *outsiders* — imprints itself on the independent present, as the family, trying to be whole, still carries the memory of the broken pattern in its psyche. Once you need your mate to pick up your toddler for you to kiss, all the while the toddler knowing it was never so before, or to lift you up the stairs, wheel you around the market — still remaining surprised at having to do these things — nothing is the same. When you cannot walk away from a marital argument, and remember the shard-like moment you knew you were burdensome, there's no balance of forces; later when you can walk, and do almost everything, you are still shadowed.

There goes your other life.

And, when they went off hiking, when I could stay back without fury — that was one stage of progress. And when they ride off into the sunset on horses, beloved horses, there will be another.

*

When they love
something tawny, lithe, rippling,
when they praise the workings
of muscle and bone, the covering
of distance, they are really praising
themselves . . .

— *from "Mistakes," Susannah Sheffer*

In parts of Montana the mountains are a dark slate-blue that stand up against the sky like elders, forbidding or generous or gentle depending on whether you feel you have pleased them. Ten years have passed since the injury, a whole decade gone in fits and starts of reinjury, partial mobility, and seismic adjustment. Two years ago, this trip would have been impossible because of the walking and sitting. (They are out riding. I am here.) In the morning, a few plump deer were munching the lawn and, as much contact with natural life feels to an urban dweller, it was like witnessing creation at the dazzling start. Out here, everyone is used to that miracle. In an exaggerated way, I was a primitive communing with these animals whose cavorting seemed so balletic. (Only the truly perverted could shoot them, unless for subsistence.) The horses my husband and daughter are riding are well cared for, and glisten like living marble with striations of sweat. The fields and meadows are parched and spiked with brown, here and there lit by yellow-green rectangles of sugar beet crops.

This is what I do: watch, admire. This is logging country; the cutting ratchety noise of saws and the sharp, piney smell of it is everywhere in these almost desolate towns. With warnings to eastern environmentalists everywhere ("We do not support animal rights activists" and "This is a household supported by logging"), it's full of exotica, such as a seminar on elk-bugling, a "testicle festival" (Bring the whole family! What this means, I think, is a Rocky Mountain oyster festival). And beauty is sprawling everywhere, spread out by a fat rough brush, with horses fitting tight to the landscape like a natural animal bloom. Horses everywhere — roans, Appaloosas, pintos — flicking flies and watching for ground squirrels, their rumps shining as they graze.

Horses: as this landscape is panoramic and dreaming inward like an animal itself, so the flanks of a horse were once to me a whole landscape. I was lost in that *lithe rippling* place of belonging. Was I indeed praising myself, admiring myself in the steaming beauty as in that poem? I was not the girl in a velvet hat with jodhpurs at the polo club, just a lover easily requited by the responsiveness of any Beauty, black or pinto or palomino. It was my competence and the incarnate grace of riding, with the power to move a larger beast, the power of love asexual and seemingly protean. With heels and the muscular press of knees and kindness, I owned a whole fine world that girls can own, though I owned no horse, just gently leading hands and strength.

Now I do not own that world, not in this family outing where two do one thing together and one observes, theirs a macro-vision of vast wildness, and mine the vista of close scrutiny. While they ride, I envy riding, but without the sting of Pilgrim Heights, or when my husband taught my daughter to water-ski, or when they both climbed a foothill that gave out at the top to a galactic scattering of lake islands gone brilliant with mist, a vista to be witness to. Now I can walk short distances without pain, sit, and even lope, a sort of clumsily sped-up walking (to escape, for instance, an orange snake yesterday), and their activities seem extraneous to the elemental fact of mobility — luxuries, big extravagances. Thus there is no longing in the old forlorn way. Yesterday I walked to get milk around the corner and was queen for a day. Because my motherhood is catching up and placing equal (though who is racing?), and there is an emerging coherent design, envy is softened and lightened. Three begins to resemble a new three, a kaleidoscope with its fragments creating one design after another, but whole.

But I *want* those horses, to ride until exhaustion breaks me and everything is seen through a sweaty lens. Want, not need: I *needed* walking. I want the speed and primeval coherence of beasts who give me the illusion that I control them, though their inchoate disobedience and freedom are what appeal so deeply, as well as their tender eyes, their dreaming of mating and new grass and horse heaven.

From a chair I watch, but I am not the same woman as the one in the car in Pilgrim Heights, nor in the hospital, nor on the damp, itchy ground. I think of P. J.'s Go-Karts, just three blocks from Bear Paw Massage, and how yesterday I bent myself into one of the hot pink missiles, and slammed (slowly) around the race concourse with the others, shocking myself, thrilled, frightened of injury — with the calm mountains ranging behind us incongruously. It seemed seductive, and my child was amazed. It was safe because the rule was that cars cannot touch each other. *Are you sure you can do it?* was probably her question, and probably she felt elation for the parent not exclusively wed to quiet, contemplative activities for a change.

Now into those Mission Mountains they take off to explore the far slate-colored miles. There will be more riding off. There will be more watching of the growing-smaller riders — distant figures against the yellow, noon-bright mountain wall — black and as symbolic to me as pictographs in the caves were to the ancient chiselers. *There went the other life,* as many lives go, and here is this one, beholding the two that should be three out there. But *should* is for a primer, not an adult vocabulary, and here is this good life.

Once More to the Lake,
Once More to the Pond

(after E. B. White)

STORY, WITH LAKE BESIDE: 1983, 1993

The white heat lightning smacks the lake over and over, making the trees chartreuse, the waves white and overwrought, and the people inside the blue house frightened and intimate. For three hours, the night is cut with acidic flashes of light, the bushes torn with wind, the terrified loons and ducks swept sideways into some low-branching shelter.

They lie in each other's arms. She thinks she might be pregnant, and sees the faces of strange animals, children, relatives, lit over and over on the knotty pine walls. She has been eating one bag of gingersnaps every day, tires very easily after walking. Others used to find her stride annoyingly fast, like slow running. Now when she runs to the dock, she becomes exhausted.

Ten years later, she is sitting and paddling a canoe for the first time in many years. The paddle feels like a real tool, strong and utilitarian, as it hits the water, and her arms seem now real tools also, having grown stronger with the occasional use of a wheelchair. There's some small grace in sitting up, although she still thinks of herself as hunched and awkward. Back there on the shore, the whole population of animals, the insects, and even other people, are indifferent to this — this small miracle of sitting up, in her gut a substantial thrill, combined with agitated excitement and fear of overdoing it. She had always hated sports, but this feel of the achieving body, the lake world at her eye level, she a participant in the ritual of water. The people are quiet, the lake is murmurous.

Suddenly, like a nerve pinched many times but never having revealed its exact location, the fury breaks. She says, "Don't you have anything to say about my being out here after so many fucking years?" He hits the water hard with his paddle. *Isn't any praise enough, isn't anything fun or soft or light anymore?* As they have been so frequently confined to the small house, they are now confined to the canoe — ridiculous in all this expansive freedom of water. The woods, now *shatterable*, noisily *shatterable* with their argument, look like a haven where their shouting, their endless bitterness, could go lie down finally exhausted, but it never is exhausted, is self-replenishing. The teeth to bite with never do grow blunt.

BELOVED LAKE: 1993

The fog has hidden one side of the lake's complex face, and the trees rimming the other side seem sprayed with misty snow from an early winter, obscuring the telling details. Even so, an exotic sienna red, then various colors of orange, splurge out like shouts, and the soothing unmuted yellow oak murmurs among the conventional conifers. In front of the cove, a formally dressed, tightly wired spruce stands next to a floating oak, branching everywhere; he, the conifer, the accountant; she the gypsy, both caught dancing in place for decades, wildly incompatible, inseparable, locked to each other by proximity and intermingled root systems. This I watch, knowing the parallels in our undancing life, but knowing how disability has made me the rigid, strait-laced tree, and made you flamboyant and expansive by contrast. Classifying the trouble in a relationship — trouble that dis-ability heightens and flings at your feet like the dog's present of an old seagull — by tree types is dangerous. But isn't it better than "dysfunctional," "dysphoric"? These trees flare and retreat, with the small breezes, all the while mingling and leaning, together.

The now cleared mirror of the lake throws this tree couple back to us, doubles it in reflection so we have to think about it twice. A little farther out there are pickerel-weeds all over, with leather leaves that are like small herons with their heads lifted up; the real full-sized heron stands up among them looking exactly like a pewter-colored Brancusi. There are ducks, bobbing toys of the water, a mink occasionally, occasionally a large silver-souled fish, lounging in the deep muck: minnows, coolness, serenity. And the gritty sound of motorcycles to make for perfect misalignment.

Then there are more motorcycles in the distance, hundreds of them tearing up the gravel, "burning" the roads, reminding us of when they all converge in Laconia in the summer, when the air is cut again and again with the powerful motors of Harleys. The men (with jeans falling off their buttocks so the cracks show) look as though they are astride an untamable force, or a real stallion with a wild will; the women perky and tightened up in leather so they look like Barbie molls sitting behind their mates. They seem so happy riding together, so jaunty, like the Wild West. One summer I saw the motorcycle women standing on a balcony in nearby Meredith. With a Molson in one hand and the other forming an improbable peace sign, they all simultaneously — following some inaudible cue — opened their vests and let their breasts hang out. Are these conventional lawyers and teachers and owners of car dealerships, as some say? *To hell with you, lake lovers, elitists, leaf peepers, motorcycle voyeurs. Fuck you!* they were saying, but also, *Look at us, aren't we just fine!* What physical disinhibition, what raucous pleasure, what rude intoxicating freedom of body.

I miss them, I miss me and us before injury.

What do I feel? once asked a Brazilian man I know, *Tell me what do I feel?* he said, not yet having the exact verbal duplicate for the specific domestic longing he felt for relatives thousands of miles away. "You know," he said, "my family's over there. Far. I'm here. It's awful. Language is so hard." I said, *"You 'miss' them,"* having never been asked to tell another person the word, the exterior frame for a dense interior picture. *You miss them.* (I miss who I was to my family, to my friends, to my mate, to my child.)

Later, I miss the motorcyclists for their sharp metallic contrast to this pristine cove, this satori, a still life complete with heron, and a couple contemplating couplehood by the lake, miss the glowering and the pseudo-fierceness of the men, the sheer bravado of all the mooning bosoms, the way I miss the gone bravado of my own body, the way we used to ride into joy together — that joy seemingly *unshatterable* then, seemingly without fade or change.

Against the clearing mirror of the lake, the trees reflect the now dusky reds and bronze golds of late afternoon; the lake is fade-proof, but the woods closest to the lake are shattered with the urban *vrooms* of these tough cowboys and cowgirls on horseback. *Summertime, fall time, love and dis-love, improbable, unpredictable.*

Here, by this loved lake, there has been perfection of love, of friendship, and the inching evolution of its change; the years of long waiting for mobility; the joyful loss of that longing, as I began to walk down the stony road. Now I sit up in a canoe long enough to touch the rough leaves of that heron weed, really pickerel-weed, so close I can see the real heron breathe — until it senses the gentled canoe and lopes away on its over-large wings. I go out in the lake: a few whitish leaves are turned facedown in the water, with their brown stems up in the air like tails, like origami creatures set loose from other parts of the world to come to just this rivulet, this cove. *Beloved lake.* Being still, or being recruited into stillness, forces the hyperactive, far-ranging eye to rest quietly on detail or else ruin its own capability for clear sight, by overuse and frustration. And my hearing has sharpened too, for the said and the unsaid, in this canoe, on this water, between friends, between family members lost and found.

Can we get back what we lost? we keep asking, and go on. As the saying goes, life just keeps happening while we decide what to do next. Now I can go to many much-desired places, though not of course to the mountain everyone climbed this morning, and never to the land of riding motorcycles or dreamed-for horses, or real dancing or skating; but I am brushed with fear, like a moth against my temple, the fear of the brutality of sudden change, the mugger around the corner. Injured or not, disabled or not, many of us are weakened by the idea of losing hold of our dependable power, so that we could be whirled around, or become like those frail origami leaves. We know the body can become the boat unmoored, a casualty of itself, or a motorcycle, or a defeated heart, or wrong cells going like kudzu through the organism.

And what is truly shatterable? The peace of the usual, which is founded on body knowledge and the habitual friendly coordination of bone, muscle, nerve, neurons, mood, and cognition. Physical or mental equipoise is like the peace in the woods, which can be abruptly broken by the ping of a rifle, and then you know something gentle and good is going down. Nothing can be taken for granted; many people secretly know that. I did before, but then taking *nothing* for granted creates unquiet and disadvantage too. Everything belongs to pattern-less fate and accident — not very compassionate mothers, but mothers of us all nonetheless.

This last day, I stay at the cove of the lake, to watch nature dress up in morning brightwork, then more subtly in mauve and heron-blue for the midafternoon rites of light falling and fading, for the distant velvet of the hours past dusk. I *choose* not to go anywhere. *Choosing:* how hoped for in the past, to *choose*. And fixed still as a camera on a tripod or that heron, I began to see everything breathing at once in the sepia quiet, saw the light finally slide away like someone leaving at the back of a church. Peace and goodness, and solitude: once more to the cove of this lake, with a new smoothness of walking, patterns of watching and not, patterns of silence and shouting.

Summertime, lost summertime; and some laughter later?

Some Harley engine music that rings with ribald joy across the giving lake?

STANDING IN THE SKY: 1995

I remember this beautiful place from before, though I have never seen it, but this is not like *déjà vu*, where a kind of heated adrenaline whacks the mind in a panic to recall *when*, and *with whom* and *how*. Warming the cells like tea in honey, this remembering in a millisecond is as surprising as finding a face almost the twin of yours; excited and calm at once, you recognize the deeper colorations of an earlier self.

From the moment of arrival, this memory is dimensional and touches all senses: first the memory of a ritual pattern of meals taken here, cereal and corn and warm salted tomatoes; and then the noise of murmuring people heard close to the inner ear of recall; then seen, the shaggy Queen Anne's lace I *may* have gathered just hours before. The bed with rough blankets seems familiar with my choppy uncertain sleep, and surely at one time, someone loved me here, or will. Here we are, in two places: moved and thrilled by the bright invented past, and the present transformed by a remembered unreal memory.

Someone has placed an old beveled mirror just above the picnic table on this enclosed porch, so that when you look into it, the whole roughened gold field in *back* of you is reflected along with your face. And thus you are seeing the field with your face set like a strange cameo within it, all within the mirror. Looking at the field, at your face, you can hear the real field breathing and languishing and basking behind you, and simultaneously smell its warmth, so there is more to mix with the pigment of the "created" remembering first felt, after the two-hour drive up. (My first long-distance drive in eight years by myself: in order to drive two hours I stopped three or four times, resting reclined for half-hour stints, making the drive four hours, the mathematics of this stage of mobility and adventure.)

There are three small rooms at this "camp" that my friend joyfully rents long-term in the summer, and a kitchen with an ancient grandmother sink, wearing its old cotton apron around steel legs, and the porch that views the sunlit, starlit, noisy-with-insects, blueberry-blotched meadow. Seamlessly, the structure fits on the edge of this field like a graft that has been taken up perfectly by the expansive mounded body of nature. Or were house and fields born together, with these natural few acres heating up and rippling in high August like desire?

Summertime: summer has become corporeal and taken root here, the word becoming this fleshy meadow, these long-limbed grasses, this sun like a voluptuous heart the color of egg yolk. And each time the people who love it here come, they distill, they capture *without taking* a part of it, almost as though joy pulled from here adds to its ecology, crucial to balanced persistence.

"Let's go swimming," I propose, even though it's dark out, a rich humus. "Are you sure?" these friends ask, disbelieving, so accustomed to "invalid" caution, a lack of physicality and adventure; I had lost the latter so long ago that they hardly recognize it in me. Their surprise is invigorating, challenging. It's as though I had suggested skydiving, rock climbing.

It is black out, with night flyers, mosquitoes and a few bats too, and inky shapes of unknown, suddenly mysterious trees that withdraw into a communal privacy at night. We will need to take the car down the short road to the murky pond because, though I feel like a roadrunner, I can't walk *that* far yet.

We emerge from the car, dark figures in old bathing suits, wandering like aliens in *Close Encounters,* holding and swaying our brilliant flashlights around the scruffy landscape. *What shall we abduct? The pond?* Too heavy, this muddy pond; in fact the dark is almost muddy, as though the night is both element and cover, like a heavy damask curtain in an old theater. Not enough light to trace a clear way; on the other hand, no canes, no crutches, no helping arms, no patronizing stares, no — help. Some tremolo of anxiety — fear of falling, tripping, going insane from outdoors elation, falling and not getting up again — is with me. Realistically, I *could* trip; the path is complex with weeds, underbrush, stones, and scurrying animal life. *Onward: one must march toward new freedom, march.*

We are not being safe. We cannot judge depth, swimming at night. Strangers in trucks rove around the road close by. They can see us, hear us, imagine us: women swimming alone, vulnerable. Who are we? Will they come back to find out?

Black night, black toes in warm primordial mud: we look up at the unsettled, slightly phosphorescent sky. In noisy hieroglyphics we write our pleased and astonished voices on the silence, on the surfaces that waver on the flat black pond. Meanwhile, our bodies seek the shallow amniotic heat of the water, go deeper in, are accepted, blessed, and baptized, born again to self-consciousness, or consciousness that our bodies are separate from the water. We scream: Is that a beaver or rat or mouse whooshing through the bushes? Is that the third time the orange truck has been this way?

If there is a true, verifiable antithesis to the hospital rehabilitation pool, here it lives in this small pond. Here we are, outside, and endangered perhaps, but only by externals: suddenly deeper water, strangers, animals. There, in the hospital pool, we were all inside much of the time, endangered by our own physiological damages, and the anguish that roved through daily life. Here in New Hampshire, the teeming natural matrix, the bugs and slimy weeds and slurpy, unpredictable bottom; there, excessive chlorine, concrete block walls where someone had optimistically (and crazily) painted a tropical scene complete with sun, pastel umbrella, beach. Where the low drone of hope and withheld hope was spoken by patients to therapists, laughter was the karate chop to pain. On this pond we now quietly breathe human and animal scent, blending into the wildness, the odor of nature, wet bodies and hair, musky and sweet and timeless. Comforting, measured against what I smelled and stared at in that other pool: terror and sadness pushed to the edge, obedience to a strict physical regime, the five steps that I could barely climb in order to get out of the water. And through it all, the plaintive talk of cure and doctors and exercises.

How could I be standing here, reader, on my own two feet in 1994, third year of gentle walking, year of mud in between the toes of the foot that joins the leg that holds the back of the horizontal woman who is upright under the hot night sky? And I initiated it? Mirabile dictu.

*

Later the moon plumps itself up in a turbulent ocean-colored sky, as though the sky could *be* the ocean, and we could walk along some ribbony boardwalk to get there and go swimming too. In fact, the sky *becomes* the ocean, with fish-stars and coral-stars and seaweed-stars, and real stars like white pebbles, and the moon swims there in that tidal firmament, with the smoldering, white-orange globularity of itself. Here we stand on the hallowed ground of the field, which is now like a sky drifted over with spiky fragrant stars that are really wildflowers and blueberry bushes and strawberries and asters. We stand and wait for something, like a constellation waiting to be named; three friends, three women in the field of middle age, by turns cynical and hopeful, but persistent in goodwill and a passionate need to still things, hold them, recreate them. Accidentally together in the long expanse of this swimming night, standing in the meadow "sky," small figures under the churning ocean above . . . This gifted summer night is to remember when hope is on its knees.

Oddly, my grandfather appears, stern and showing off again; there he is in the cloud waves of the ocean the sky has become, standing on his head on an aquaplane behind a motorboat at fifty-five, sixty, seventy years old. He's waving. Physical prowess has always had an extreme edge of folly and danger in my family. (It only makes symmetrical sense that the disabled one would be extreme too, that "temporary" would become eight years.) He continues aqua-planing, on his way toward death.

Now it's getting crowded here.

A little off to the side in the meadow is another presence lying on a white lawn chair, like the fourth point of the constellation, but she is not gently flickering. She burns like the red warning lights of a vehicle. This burning mixes with the heat of her volition; she lies under the sky-ocean and looks up at the great cold distance between her and radiance. (And farther back in the room of the cabin is another weepy, earlier aspect of her, resentful and pretending not to be, enviously waiting for the swimmers, the ones who Left Her All Alone.) Set against our robustness, the seeming effortlessness of our standing there, the one in the chair speaks through a gray muslin, the chill of exclusion seeping into her, newly angry again. *When do I get to stand up and walk? I can't get to the pond,* she churns, unloving, furious. (Be quiet for a while, I tell her, looking back at her incendiary eyes.)

She lives in me always. But she is not as powerful or mysterious as the lunar hand that now moves in great ripples over the field, fingering flowers and weeds, and breaking against the stars of our newly configured constellation. It moves against our legs and pushes rough stalks against our calves, our receptive skin, our combined strength. *Peace and goodness,* and standing without help — nothing to lean on, nothing to prop me up — in a field in New Hampshire.

Girl with Bird, in Bronze

Suddenly, I realize
That if I stepped out of my body, I would break
Into blossom.

— from "A Blessing," James Wright

She is quiet in her bronze skin, the curve of her spine bending perfectly over the common sparrow in her hand, whispering to it, coaching it to fly or eat. She is a configuration of aesthetic and human traits, the one aspect shaped with knowing, artistic hands, the other with a heart for hammering simplicity and tenderness out of cold element. Untended, her fountain is almost dry; the few inches of water are as brown as tea, and drifted over with candy wrappers, tree debris, Popsicle sticks.

"Look," I tell my daughter and my friend, "how she seems to talk to this bird." *Look how I am standing here, nine years later: how could this be?*

I have arrived at her feet with my happily working legs. Welcome to this seed, the girl says to the bird. Welcome to the walking world, I say to myself, looking around uncertainly with my now tall, now independent child beside me. *How did you get so big I'll never be able to pick you up again?*

And welcome to delivery of a splendor the body barely remembers or recognizes. Within the silent memory of sockets, tendons, and muscles, there was mostly labor and hurt: holding tight to walking bars, reinjury, more therapy, more setbacks. But this is splendor in a small distance covered, in smooth uncerebrated motion: Is this akin to what a baby feels, arms stretched out, finally the real conqueror of a wide world?

*

Like Magellan, I had looked across the hazy oceanic stretch of the Boston Public Garden, unfathomable and long — as long as a city block seemed to stretch three years ago, as the miles from the front door to the driveway looked six years ago, as the dining room seemed from the kitchen at first. Yet I was going to walk across it, easing myself in as though into water, joining atoms with other leisurely atoms; becoming background, then foreground, background, foreground, thankfully as invisible as everyone else here. Nine years had passed since the original injury; during that time I resembled the ape figure on the evolution chart, except I started flat, and inched toward mobility year by year, finally emerging upright and victorious. Uneasily and slowly, I was now stepping into the *concept* of a walking body, and that body was blooming out of its old injured wood like Daphne. And as Daphne, as Magellan, as the once horizontal woman, my destination became the garden's other side, where the bronze "Girl with Bird" lives mesmerized, in her own bronze time.

A double image, this body-turned-into-blossoming on the already blossoming garden, wanton with color, though formal. My own bloom is private, wild; I had been locked in a bronze of solid pessimism, based on years of sliding backward, with slight progress followed by failure and recuperative confinement, followed by the lure of progress again in a punishing cycle, so familiar to long-term convalescence. Now I was up! *Who are you, woman, to be so uncontainable? How can you be so thrilled with such small distance?* To be walking again is over the brim of happiness. This near mania has accompanied every piece of rehabilitation: going to the movies, out to dinner after four years, sitting up for an hour, taking my daughter to shop. Here is the body engaging in its manifest destiny as a smoothly working thing. After atrophy and disuse, and the conviction that *never* would I walk this far again, my legs are like two exclamation points that follow sentences about them. I break into blossom: *I can do it. Can't I do it. Can. Can.*

Beside me is the horizontal woman, always, pentimento under the moving canvas, lively ghost.

The Swan Boats slide by, stately and frivolous. Behind a scrim of memory, two women — my mother and I — try to get a bulky rickety wheelchair across the garden to the Swan Boats so that I can join the anonymous ranks of active recreational people. The quest had been to fit in everywhere; whereas in fact I fit nowhere, no one could see what was wrong. On that day, however, we had wheeled past the homeless sleeping on their favored nesting benches, the drunks confabulating all day long, and the crazy ones begging in tongues from the high-spirited garden-goers. It was too blatant a reversal: my mother pushing, me being pushed, anger keeping me from seeing or entering the garden.

Now I am about the same height as everyone else; I am conventional and I blend into the diorama of spring. No one smiles pityingly, yet I remember the secret unacknowledged inequality of being pushed in a wheelchair, where one person is seemingly fit and strong, and one seemingly weak. (I speak only for my own state: perhaps for those who have never walked, or who have a long time to adapt, and more fortitude, not walking loses its scalpel edge and the public gaze becomes invisible.) But those years of limitations in the tall swift world were flooded with a yearning for mobility that omnivorously took pleasure from other activities.

I think others are stronger and more obdurate. But what are their private strifes, their imperfect adjustments and dreams to be otherwise? That young woman in the wheelchair over by the statue of George Washington has joy and pride in her bearing, but it cannot be all bravery and strength, as the activists want; difference hurts, *not walking* hurts. What is her interior life? For our society is based on motion, defines us partly by walking. It likes what fits in seamlessly, likes the decisive action that accompanies motion, disdains an Eastern kind of stillness, wants fast productivity above all, despite spates of goodwill and protestations to the contrary. In fact, the biblical definition of being human, as opposed to sky or river or animal, is phrased as *the ones who have dominion over the ones that are closer to the ground.* Given this, it's no wonder that the depression which accompanies loss of uprightness is amplified by unjust, inbred societal expectations.

Motion and speed are common indices of power, definition — even commitment. Walkathons are the main gesture of charity and compassion of the eighties and nineties; we prove how much we care by the distances we cover. And our vocabularies are full of powerful walking themes; "walking tall" is being full of pride or honor. "Walk of life" defines social class or occupation. "Walking papers": discharge or dismissal phrased by the dramatic metaphor of walking. Moonwalking. Crosswalk. Walk softly and carry a big stick. Just walk out. Walk, don't run. Walking in a Winter Wonderland. Take a walk, man. Just walk a mile in his boots before you criticize him. These Boots Were Made for Walking. Just a Closer Walk with Thee. (And what about those who cannot, either temporarily or permanently? How close can they get to Thee?) For He walks with me and He talks with me. Walkman. Walkwoman. Woman walking, woman not walking, woman walking again, and grateful.

Who am I? I used to ask. What had I become to others in the glaring standing-up world? (I had no idea.) Who was I, naked without the cloth of my familiar, cozy physical self? Disorienting, overly mysterious to myself, lonely, floundering. Subtract the joyful physicality from mothering suddenly, and then what? Subtract free-ranging ability — in employment and consumerhood and most roles — and the free-ranging spirit feels subtracted too. In veterans' hospitals everywhere, in rehab hospitals and psych units and single-room hotels, the toll of extreme subtraction is evident. Mine was temporary, comparatively minor; people who can add help to their lives can soften the subtraction. In truth, an upright "normal" person is easily embraced by society; "fallen" people become outsiders whom society would rather not notice, even as it stares. Although people with all kinds of disabilities have forced the larger so-called normal culture to modify preferences and get to work on changing the desire for sameness in physicality, the preference for perfect function remains in attitude, vocabulary, and in that certain odd pitying smile.

*

"Do you want to rest?" my friend asks, as we spot a wedding, also planted wildly in this garden. *Does this count as a real walking triumph, if I stop to rest?* The bride and groom, in red and white — a wedding postponed from December? — and all twenty attendants are yanked from noisy animation into still, stiff smiling by the photographer, who arranges their faces into ricti. The women all in slightly different dresses turn into an almost symmetrical tableau: The Wedding Pose. *Caution, Go Slow, Danger Ahead,* I say, doubt and cynicism almost a metal ore in the personality now, knowing how the scissor god can snip at any picture full of relationship and cut it into dry shreds. Like others who deal with chronic physical problems, or profound stress, my husband and I have sifted through these shreds for years; we have tried to make it through a domestic day in truce, in quiet, when the high noise of pain makes the nerves dance constantly and the self go haywire. Now the scissors are momentarily laid aside. Good luck to them: the bride's head tilts, the groom looks up, as much as the bird looks to the Bronze Girl.

"*Onward to see her,*" I announce. Why does this voyage matter so much? Do I get a prize, do all my physical therapists "win"? Do I still need to count the stages of recovery; line up my debits (still some pain, still the white chair, still the cane) and credits (stood in line for ten minutes, climbed two flights of stairs, walked across the Public Garden)? I am still justifying progress and discounting the amazing unrealistic dreams others had for me when I wanted only *to walk* without pain, fear reduced to a small hum. *(I think you should set your hopes higher. Climbing Mount Monadnock or maybe running around the block. You could someday, I bet.)* All my goals were small and sweet: navigating on my own, and the plainsong of walking this far with my now tall daughter beside me. The horizontal woman reminds me that my child can't be as happy for me, for us, as I am; she can't be steamrolled into this kind of ecstasy. While I want her to celebrate progress, it might make her travel to the past too much: Who knows what harsh edges her long, precise memory has? For now, mother and daughter just walk toward a small sculpture.

This is Eden in the walking garden, the egalitarian public garden, where the earthly delights are whatever you name them: beer on the grass, dowager jewelry brought out just for the spring promenade down Newbury Street, the rich green crew-cut grass underfoot on a half day out of a halfway house, a first or last ride on the Swan Boats.

The bronze girl, whose wavy hair gleams in the spring air, is closer now. She was cast in 1917 by Buska Paeff, a twenty-one-year-old immigrant, who first modeled small clay figures while selling tickets at a Boston subway station. This girl deserves eternity; recast three times after theft and vandalism, she is eerily familiar, like a distillate of childhood, or fictive childhood. Girl with Bird, you are found again, with my earned strange miles of walking across the green ocean: you are the muse of bronze.

And the bronze will turn out really to be *Boy with Bird*, but not for me. She is always Eve's girl child in the garden, the unrecorded, ephemeral offspring born in Eden. Did she ever presume to be a destination to anyone, or the zenith of a blossoming? Buska Paeff, as you cast, did you imagine what mirrors of revelation would melt together in this sculpture, what hungers for flight or feeding would be provoked by the evanescence called Bird? Thousands have found their own childhoods here, its losses and affinities, beauty or impoverishment.

The homeless lie near her, propped on the stone ledge where it is dry; the drunks and crazies pray in front of her: "Mother, Sister, Father, Sergeant, Sister Mary." I will touch her arm, not for luck, as the Florentines touch the Porcellino's shiny nose, but for commemoration of her persistence through time and theft and pollution: daughter of the garden.

I never knew that my yearned-for Eden was the simple ability to walk, sit up to write a paragraph, stand to wash a dish, to wave good-bye. But my own body threw me out, a fact still grievous because it was not a result of taking health risks, not from volition, not for Rabelaisian living. And the garden becomes whatever we have lost; what Adam and Eve lost in Genesis was intimacy with the divine, and so they went on looking for it. In the real and gritty garden with stoplight-red tulips and duck shit and condoms and swans, I know that one dramatic expulsion is sudden or drawn-out estrangement from normalcy, from intimacy with the familiar use of self, and that the ensuing wilderness stretching before the mind has few boundaries.

Though not in the usual agnostic vocabulary, sin and *without* (Latin *sine*) have always been associated for me. Expelled, Adam and Eve were *without* God, outside of the garden, separate from all else created so far. Following this twisted theological path, being without much mobility gave me a visceral sense of being cast out (losing caste, too) and with it the bewilderment of shame. Shame: Who would ever imagine it alive alongside the bad luck of injury, or illness, or accident? This day is ripe with spring, but the remembered *shame* of feeling *ashamed* covers like the caul that the horizontal woman lived in. Do others ever feel it? The question is difficult to ask. No one wants to admit shame.

No advocate would want me to say it, but when people stared, I often could not boldly repudiate them by staring back or challenging. (And why? I was tired. I was not able. I felt shame at being stared at. I was mute with the dailiness of just getting by. Advocacy and self-defense are depleting. Gazing back was sometimes too difficult on difficult days.) Regardless of intent, age, or demeanor of the starers, I felt stripped of dignity under the strobe of their scrutiny: shame around which Ingmar Bergman made a whole movie. But Erik Erikson comes closest to understanding: "Shame supposes that one is being completely exposed and conscious of being looked at . . . one is visible and not ready to be visible." Being singled out, looked at without permission; that's the not ready to be visible part. Think: the bronze girl has always to be ready, the offspring of time. She is art, meant to be displayed. Most people will not display themselves voluntarily. True that when a woman lies down wherever she is, just because there's nowhere else for her, it's unusual; people are understandably curious, put off. High visibility makes anyone a target. But the stares would continue relentlessly, even with the cane, and eventually there's both acute self-consciousness and an impotence: *Can you stop now, please?*

> *Me:* What are you thinking when you stare at me?
> *Starer:* I'm glad, you know, that I don't have to use a wheelchair. But you *look* fine.
> *Me:* I don't use it all the time. (I'm not fine.)

Starer: No way *any*time for me, and how could you possibly lie down in a filthy bus station like this?

Me: It's hard to sit up, so after the wheelchair, I have to lie down: what's my choice, if I'm to go anywhere?

But if I was going to do more than stay at home and grow neurotic roots there, if I was going to raise my child *in* the world, I had to go public, go visible, even though absorbed in the new privacy of my capsized self. But no one had my permission to make me an object of judgment. I wanted that privacy, that border between my country and theirs. But in spite of desiring to recede, I was the one who inevitably emerged to the foreground of scenes, grabbing attention. Others thought I was ill, tired, drunk on the floor. Shame was planted; it grew, though the wish was for it to turn to pride, or sassiness, or bravado.

Now in this garden, no one stares, unless they are fine-tuned to ecstacy; or unless they love to watch friendship and maternity glow with usage.

Halfway across, the sunlit wind picks up one of the strange stiff bouquets from the wedding, and lifts it like a flowered bird. The Swan Boats insist on spring; the rehab always insisted on fall and winter. When I walk I will always remember not walking. The bronze head of the girl becomes very visible now, and momentarily the consciousness of walking fades; I pull up short and guilty, as though I must always bear the past in mind, the joints silently rebellious on misfitting hinges. *Remember! Or you won't be able to walk,* I say, a kind of charm against recurrence. *Watch out. Take nothing for granted.* The strange wedding behind us carries the canvas of its possible dissolution, the bride and groom walking away to opposite ends of the garden. Walking now, there is still yearning for walking, damnit.

Everywhere people are complimenting gypsy spring for its usual display of wares. Wanting to be those people once turned into envy, even hate, for what they took so for granted, enjoying movement and uprightness, the natural evolutionary stance of humans. Just as waves come in and out and the weather changes, walking and sitting and standing were theirs to have *without cherishing*. For their not cherishing it, I had been angry, especially as people picked up children, hugged each other, leaped out of danger, helped each other with groceries. Bitterness grew: the active part of the best job I ever had, late motherhood, was lost and mourned, until bitterness was almost the taste of everything. I came to understand how it deforms some people so others can't stand them; why a blind person who does *not* want help crossing the street furiously shakes his cane. No matter what the *inability* or specific *anger*, to feel weak or dependent at once is depleting, as though the world is giant and strong, and you are forced backward, lilliputian.

*

"Can you believe it?" I ask my daughter, who has turned to the exciting spectacle of the noisy, high-spirited wedding. "Can you imagine what this means to me?" Too insistently, I threw the same question at my friend who *can* imagine, more than most, because she drove my daughter home from day care every day for four months, seeing my overly eager face at the window, as I waited for the returning child to redeem the glassy boredom of another claustrophobic day inside. Now they both smile, but they do not enter the acres of my opening universe. Having always been someone for whom everything is discussable, I know now there is a kind of silence — as self-contained as the bronze girl — that replaces word or gesture or physical affection. We are all quiet.

For some joy is not to be shared, not to be rendered down to a pool of expressed emotion. It bends over language, and the self bows down to it in serious awe. Walking in the garden is *my* earthly delight — the "gardenous world," as the poet Gerald Stern calls it. For some, this moment in the scattering urban light is like many others in the collection called "Day"; for me on this particular one, brightness does fall from the air, saturating all in the thick gold of spring heat. For now, the exile of the body is partly over, though the spiritual education by exile will not end. There is a chance, the horizontal woman knows, I know, of debilitation again; reels of horizontalism are carried inside like a silent movie, with grays too dark and the whites too raw and bright. But there she is, and I am, in front of the girl/boy with the tamed bird, the air running like a river of silk around us. With my own loving girl beside me, I take step after step into a new world, wild and joyous and fearful with possibility.